Edward Bradbury

In the Derbyshire Highlands

Highways, Byeways, and My Ways in the Peake countrie

Edward Bradbury

In the Derbyshire Highlands
Highways, Byeways, and My Ways in the Peake countrie

ISBN/EAN: 9783744772983

Printed in Europe, USA, Canada, Australia, Japan

Cover: Foto ©Andreas Hilbeck / pixelio.de

More available books at **www.hansebooks.com**

IN THE
DERBYSHIRE
HIGHLANDS:

HIGHWAYS, BYEWAYS, AND MY WAYS IN THE PEAKE COUNTRIE.

BY

EDWARD BRADBURY.

("STREPHON.")

AUTHOR OF "PILGRIMAGES IN THE PEAK," &c., &c.

BUXTON: J. C. BATES.
LONDON AND DERBY: BEMROSE AND SONS;
SHEFFIELD: PAWSON AND BRAILSFORD;
CHESTERFIELD: WILFRED EDMUNDS.

1881.

[*All Rights Reserved.*]

To
William Black,

In Admiration of His Genius,
In Remembrance
Of Some Pleasant Hours Passed
In His Society in the Western
Highlands, and
In Gratitude
For His Kindly Counsels,
This Little Wayside Wildflower,
Grown Outside the Garden of
Literature,
Is Offered.

CONTENTS.

CHAP.		PAGE
I.	ROUND BY THE ROACHES, WITH A LOOK AT LUDCHURCH	1
II.	THE VALLEY OF THE GOYT	32
III.	CLIMBING COOMBS MOSS	48
IV.	AN EXCURSION TO ERRWOOD	65
V.	A DERBYSHIRE VALLEY IN THE SPRING TIME	77
VI.	AT CHANTREY'S GRAVE	92
VII.	OVER THE HIGH PEAK RAILWAY	104
VIII.	IN THE KINDERSCOUT COUNTRY	121

CHAP.		PAGE.
IX.	Round and About Buxton	161
X.	Chatsworth as a Treasure-House of Art	188
XI.	Haddon Hall: An Autumnal Vignette	221
XII.	Hunting in the High Peak	227
XIII.	A Cruise Round Castleton	239

TO THE READER.

THE majority of the papers in the present volume appeared in the *Derbyshire Times* under the title of "Undiscovered Derbyshire." The exceptions are the articles on Chatsworth and Haddon Hall, which are republished from *The Magazine of Art*, with the kind consent of Messrs. Cassell & Co. The public favour which followed the appearance of the "Undiscovered Derbyshire" series has been a sufficient inducement for their transfer from newspaper columns to these pages. "Undiscovered Derbyshire" was meant to be, as the title portended, an index to the less known and little explored 'beauty-spots' of the Peake district—the sweet dells, and hidden nooks, and moorland wilds—which lie just off the beaten road, and which, though so remote, are quite near to the tourist path. Most of the places described therein are within the proverbial stone's-throw of Buxton; some, indeed, are only an idle afternoon's excursion from the Crescent.

To the Genius of the Guide Book these modest touch-and-go sketches have no pretence; yet sufficient accuracy and attention to detail are observed to enable the reader to follow with facility the footsteps of the writer.

In anticipation of shrewd criticism hinting, with a nudge of superior wisdom, that several of the places mentioned in these pages are not in Derbyshire at all, but belong to Staffordshire or Cheshire, the author would submit beforehand that the Peake Countrie should not be called upon to scrupulously toe an arbitrary topographical line; and he would meekly suggest that when the wayward wanderings of a mountain stream, or the curves of a lonely valley, take the reader on to the borderlands, he need not dispute the landmark of county demarcation, like an ordnance surveyor, a litigious landowner, or a haggling Highway Board.

But these "tiny travels" off the beaten track are not likely to send mankind into convulsions of controversy; and, perhaps, so small a volume scarcely required so large a preface.

STREPHON.

DERBY, 1881.

ROUND BY THE ROCHES,

WITH A LOOK AT

LUDCHURCH.

*Come, let us to the hills! where none but God
Can overlook us; for I hate to breathe
The breaths and think the thoughts of other men
In close and crowded cities, where the sky
Frowns like an angry father mournfully.
I love hills and I love loneliness,
And oh! I love the woods, those natural fanes
Whose very air is holy; and we breathe
Of God; for He doth come in special place,
And, while we worship, He is there for us.*
                                    FESTUS.

"FIFTY, fifty-seven; fifty-two, fifty-seven!" It is a tournament under the gas-light. The combatants have their coats off, and are tilting with pointed lances, which they ever and anon render deadly with chalk. The spectators sit on seats raised above the cloth of green. There is no Queen of Beauty, but an automatic herald, in the evening dress indispensable to the successful waiter, proclaims the issues: "Fifty-nine, fifty-three."

The scene is the billiard-room of a Buxton hotel where "Kalmat" and myself have been driven by stress of rain, which is making the Spa of the Peak more than ever a "watering-place." The weather does not look auspicious for a Pilgrimage in the Peak to Ludchurch and the Roches, which we have planned for to-morrow. The pluvian deities seem to have set their faces against "Kalmat"—a wanderer in many lands—seeing a little of the neglected scenery of his own country. "Kalmat" had never heard of Ludchurch. He asked whether it belonged to the Anglican Establishment, and his ignorance of the Roches is as dense as a London fog. Buxton is crowded with visitors. The "season" is at its height. How many of the people—educated Englishmen—visiting the North Midland Spa, I wonder, have ever heard of our shrine? Were Buxton threatened with the fate of Sodom and Gomorrah, and the condition of deliverance that peradventure ten men should be found who knew Ludchurch and the Roches, the fashionable *sanatorium* would be doomed to the condign destruction of the wicked cities of the plain. There is no part of England less known than the heathery highlands half-a-dozen miles from Buxton, where Staffordshire and Cheshire and Derbyshire meet in a wild solitude whose scenery haunts the senses like a spell. These highlands of England have yet to be discovered. They are very near civilization, and still very far from it. They are not on the beaten track. They are off the rail. The guide-books know them not. The Royal Engineers could not find Ludchurch. You may scrutinise the ordnance map in vain to find indication of that solemn temple. We know more of the sources of the Nile, and of the North Pole, than of this "backbone of England." Unexplored Derbyshire is as far away from the ordinary Englishman as the *terræ incognitæ* of equatorial Africa. We are wonderfully intimate with lands thousands of miles away, but we are strangely ignorant, and scandalously neglectful, of the "beauty-spots" in our very midst, next door to us, in the same parish, so to speak. The nearest to us is the most remote. What is easily reached is lightly prized. The accessible is not attractive; the nearest is not always the dearest. Scenery, like the prophet, hath no honour in its own country. "Why Ludchurch is only eight miles from Buxton!" exclaimed the late Duke of Westminster to one of many parties he was driving from Eaton Hall to Ludchurch, and he spoke with the suddenness accompanying a startling discovery.

Over supper our prospects for the morrow seem damp and dubious, and a certain Potentate in Petticoats, who will not be able to accompany us, throws

even more cold water on the scheme . . . . .
But lo! this morning there is a radiance in the air; the sky has a blueness that might have been borrowed from Italy; the sun lights up the landscape. Mornings of such brilliant promise are often disappointing as they grow older. The glory is too great to last. Like the majority of Senior Wranglers, such days put forth all their brightness into their early history. The maturity is common place; the eventide even mournful. But to-day the promise of the morning will be fulfilled throughout, for behold! the cattle are grazing on the tops of the hills, outlined forms sketched against the sky, surest sign of continued fineness, as the farmers, who know nothing about meteorology, but a great deal about the weather, will tell you.

The breakfast bells are ringing at Buxton, as we are driving out of the town. There is a sweet strong air that has kissed the heather; a thin, buoyant atmosphere that laces the nerves like a "pick-me-up." Up hill and past Burbage, where the lime-burners until recently lived in burrows, like ancient cave-men, and then all that tells of man and mammon all that is connected with the selfish gain and greed and care, and "gin and steam-hammers," of the nineteenth century is left behind. We are driving on the Leek-road. It winds along the purple slopes of Axe Edge. The moors encompass us. On the hill-side are two rustic bilberry gatherers. A study for Birkett Foster that bare headed boy with the blue eyes and flaxen curls, and frank fresh face, and corduroy trousers, patched at the knee, that button on to his long-sleeved waistcoat; with his earnest little sister, whose brown hands are stained with the juice of the jet-beaded fruit. A picture in herself, this little mountain maiden, in her rude rush hat, unribboned save by the sunlit wind-blown tresses of her hair, and the red roses of her bonny cheeks.

In front, lying in a world of silence and solitude, rise a company of peaked hills: some with the sun catching their grassy slopes and touching them with a tenderer green; others with a gray veil of mist hanging down their shoulders, a pugaree to keep the sun from their necks. That pyramidical mountain is Croom Peak; the hill whose shape suggests a sugar-loaf is Parker's Hill; the elevated ridge on the left of the blade-like contour of Axe Edge is Wild Boar Clough, where the last wild boar in England was hunted to the death; the peak that keeps it company is Shutlings Low. One or two white farmhouses, with a blue film rising from their chimneys, the very poetry of smoke, are scattered in the grey gritstone hollows. Vivid patches of green among the dark heath show where a crop of late hay has been gathered. It is "high farming" in these parts; but not the scientific agriculture of Mr. Mechi. Rather the farming of Virgil's time. Steam and phosphates are as remote from the mind of the Hodges of these highlands as they were from Triptolemus, with his primitive plough and yoke of bullocks. This stubborn land in niggard spaces reclaimed from the moors, is not exactly the earth that Jerrold described which, when tickled with a hoe, laughed with a harvest. Still I have heard of farmers in these lonely latitudes obtaining two crops of oats in one year; one in January and one in October. It was because the oats of the September of one year were not harvested until the January of the next year. "Wild oats," indeed. "Kalmat" is opposed to any attempt being made to reclaim the moors. He says the heath retains moisture, and that the moors are the natural watersheds of the country, and that cultivation would cut off the water-supply. But remember "Kalmat" is a sportsman.

A strong light lies on the nearer moorland, bringing out an opulency of purple, save where a passing argosy of pearly cloud sails in soft slow advancement of shade over the pronounced brightness; but far away in the silent loneliness, where the wide distant sea of heather melts into the sky, there is a sunny haze of delicate tints, amethysts, opals, and tender greys, blended in a dream of colour. And all around is the spell of silence, the sense of space, the scent of thyme and heather. Once or twice there is the sudden whir-r-r of a grouse; once or twice the reverberating ping of the breechloader is heard, and sportsman and smoking tube of steel are seen in relief against the sky, a sharp silhouette.

Pause awhile charioteer at this isolated group of white, wayside cottages. This is Dove Head. Close by the roadside is the spring of the river Dove, rising from the great water-shed of Axe Edge. A lichened stone bears the initials of Izaak Walton and Charles Cotton, entwined in a moss-grown monogram. The two Piscators often tasted the water of their beloved stream at this spot. The water is as pure and sweet now as when the two classic brothers of the angle walked these dales, fishing through all the stormy troubles of the Civil War, and caring as little for King or Commonwealth as Canning's needy knife-grinder cared for politics. Thanks for the cup of your pocket flask. And now, Sir, my service to you. One of the most enchanting walks of these islands is to keep company with the "princess Dove" from this spring; to woo her in all her winsome, wayward course; to listen to her song amid the rocky romance of Dove Dale, and to linger by her side through great breadths of green until the sheeny river flies to the broad bosom of the Trent. Someday, Kalmat, we will make the excursion.

It is not far from Dove Head to Flash. Whoever heard of Flash? Yet this grey, gritstone village, lost among the moors, has given the English language an expressive synonym. Spurious coin in the "good old days" was minted here; the people were as uncouth as the country; and the inaccessible village was the scene of many pugilistic encounters. Flash is, in fact, the debatable land that borders equally upon Staffordshire, Derbyshire, and Cheshire. So it was easy for members of the P.R. to laugh at the law by stepping from the jurisdiction of one county into that of another, should the constabulary of one district interfere with their fistic art. There is, indeed, a story told of a worthy J.P. of a past decade being apprised of a great battle-royal between the Burslem Bruiser and the Preston Pet. Coming down with some friends to see the fray, he found the ring pitched within his own magisterial boundaries. He sternly ordered the fighting fraternity off the ground. They obediently moved a few yards further on the moor, passing over the frontier of another county. In their fresh location the stern Nemesis of the law, became the enthusiastic Mecœnas of the ring, for both the magistrate and his party remained to see the fight, and contributed towards the subscription. The present Flash is peaceable enough. It is more interested in farming than forgery, and the rowdy pugilism has given way to a pastoral quiet that is like an idyll of Theocritus.

Now, with the sweet caress of the wind in our faces, we bowl merrily along a valley between the moors. Those gritstone posts that keep repeating themselves out of the moor are the "Duke of Argyle's monuments," but they are intended for cattle and not for kilted Scotchmen. The T shaped stone structures, which would no doubt have caused much anxious speculation to the antiquarian members of the Pickwick Club, are cattle shelters, where cattle may seek protection from the hungry wind that in winter wails over these moors. Keeping us company is a burn that is a tributary of the Dane. It is a limpid mountain maiden whose life has increased from fretful infancy at our side. We heard the first note of her baby prattle among the rocks and ferns of the brae. She was fed by freshets and sung to by the wind, and then came the careless, lisping chatter of the growing girl. Now it is the musical song of the damsel of sweet seventeen, with a necklace of white water-crowfoot trembling on her breast, coquetting with hanging tree and fern and flower, as she skips from rock to rock in all the fervour of health and hope and youth and beauty. "Kalmat's" affectionate nature is in love with the singing stream. He finds meanings and modulations in its voice.

Here is Quarnford, with door-ways, windows, and dados, wearing blue facings of lime-wash. Poor cottages, but as clean and comely as those of the boasting village of Brock. There is poverty, but not squalor; and the children are characterised by that cleanliness which is the elegance of the poor. There is a Wesleyan chapel by the wayside. Wheresoever in the Peake countrie there happens to be a cluster of grey houses, huddling together as if for warmth, there is sure to be a little Bethel. The National Church at one time neglected the wilds of Derbyshire. The people grew up as savage as the country. But the fiery fervour of Wesley, and the fierce fanaticism of Whitfield, reached the heathen of these highlands, and the preaching of Methodism was as the introduction of Christianity to the benighted aborigines. Depend upon it the High Peak owes more to Wesleyan zeal than some of us imagine.

The next hamlet is Gradbach. Now our exploration must be made on foot. So our charioteer is sent away to meet us across the country some miles hence, at a hostelry among the hills called the Royal Cottage. We shall see him again in three or four hours hence. So we say. *Au revoir*, then, son of Phaeton. We are left alone amidst an amphitheatre of hill and fell, over which the sun ever and anon sends tidal waves of light, turning sober greys into intense greens, and browns into burning golds. Here purple moorland, a vast undulating breadth, a sea of waves rolling away to an ocean line on the horizon; there a clearing and a patch of ripening wheat; anon a dash of white that might be snow, but it is lime spread over the heath by the farmer persistent to kill the heather and reclaim a few acres for husbandry. Everywhere is the sound of water, the music of eager water-threads stealing out of the bank past an old farm-house, with a heap of moss-grown stones at the gate, (a horse-block for the safe mounting of fat farmer or dowdy dowager bearing heavy baskets for the market,) to the valley of the Dane, where there is a deserted old mill and one or two cottages in ruins. Upon broken window and decaying roof a curse might rest. The place seems haunted in its dark enclosure of wooded bank. The shadowy nook is the scene for a ghost-story.

And now the Mecca of our pilgrimage is nigh. The darkly wooded hill-side, sloping to the Dane, is the ancient Back Forest of Swythamley, whose yews furnished Robin Hood with hunting-bows, and where Ludchurch is hidden. Above and beyond the steep

sloping wood—Pelion piled upon Ossa—rise the
Roches, black and grim even under this blue radiancy
of sky. The crazy timbered structure we are now
crossing is Caster's Bridge. Under it the Black-
brook races past a tumult of bearded gritstone rocks
to the Dane, which, rising on the western flank of
the Axe Edge, here divides East Cheshire and North
Staffordshire, and afterwards, when its life has been
blurred and disfigured by the outrages of man, joins the
Weaver at Northwich to enter the Mersey at Runcorn.
The rough, old, moss-grown plank crossing, with the
stone harassed water racing past in a series of noisy
little waterfalls—waves of white which the sun ever
and anon strikes—is picturesque enough in its green
setting to detain a painter. But the old Caster's
Bridge of arching grey stone, long since washed
away, might have enchanted an artist hither. It
was a memory in masonry, a story in stone. Lin-
gering legends lent the quaint arch the charm
of heroic association. One of them told of a
time when a brigand's hostel stood close by, and
to which tired travellers were decoyed and mur-
dered. A weary pedlar sought a night's rest at
this sham caravansary. He saw the robbers
melting ore. And he heard these dreadful,
blood-curdling words urgently whispered: "*Mother,
when will that queer old man be dead? I'm*

sure *the oven is quite hot enough.*" The **prudent pedlar ran away with remarkable celerity for a footsore man.** Pursued, he found a narrow **ridge within the arching roof of** Caster's Bridge. The pack of murderous men **and women and dogs, who hunted** him like sleuth-hounds, **were thus** eluded. The **refugee made the** best of **his way to a** Staffordshire **town.** He gave his evidence before **the authorities.** Soldiers sacked **the** den. The desperadoes were secured. **They were** tried and hung. All this, it is true, happened " once upon a time." That, perhaps, **is all** that is true about it. There are **not even any** ruins left to mark the stage of **so much pre-Sweeny-Todd-melodrama.** Deponent says that a **flood washed the ruins away,** and **that gold has from time to time** been **discovered on the** supposed site of the razed building. "Kalmat," however, is suspicious of the story. But his companion loves the old grotesque, country-side traditions. **They are** the green oases in the arid desert of history. They **have** met with the unchallenged acceptance of succeeding generations, and have thus **a** broad base for belief. We **are too eager** to dissect and **analyse,** and follow that shrewd scientist who endeavoured to upset " Robinson Crusoe," **by** pointing out that the rice which the castaway sowed could not have grown because it had been dressed and denuded of its fructifying properties.

The surrounding scene is picturesque enough for any romance. Walking on at issue over old legends, we are almost unconscious that we have been following a path that climbs the shadowy hillside, high above the Dane, which is now quite lost in the shade of spruce and larch and fir, and anon sends up flashes of liquid light from the wooded water-way. The river lies in a deep canon beneath. Steppes of far-reaching moorland rise up on the other side. We are in the green gloom of the Back Forest. The upward path winds through a Gothic aisle of lambent leaves. Mossy columns support the arched roof of foliage, through which the sun is reflected in light leaf-shadows on the tangled path. It is September, and the trees are tinted by the artistic touch of Autumn. Green is still the prevailing colour; but there are spots of rose-red on the knotty-boled beeches; an orange glow is spreading on the maple; the oaks are splashed with yellow and the acorns are turning brown; there is a shimmer of light yellow on the limes; the elms are fading into a soft amber; the chestnut has a bronzed gleam; the tresses of the birch are of a golden hue. The mountain ash blazes with clusters of vivid red beads; there are bright coral berries on the hip bushes; wild raspberries impede our progress; the yellow and white waxwork petals of the scented woodbine stretch across the narrow path. There is an ungathered bouquet of wild blue-bells and streaked convolvuses yet remaining of the summer, and a wealth of golden gorse, which flowers in every season. The nuts on the hazel boughs are racing the blackberries into ripeness; the haws are reddening on the thorn. There is a harmony of hue; chord of colour answers chord. This secluded depth of forest might almost be the home of Pan. Mr. Ruskin once said that in the valley of the Derbyshire Wye you might expect to catch sight of the Arcadian God and the Muses. And here in this wild-wooded solitude, as we sit awhile on a cushion of moss with our pipes amid the fragrance of the resinous pines, in a silent session of thought, the sigh of a falling leaf is like the gentle movement of a dryad, and that blue-bell, whose chalice is catching the sunlight, might be the azure gaze of some retiring faun; and the Dane where the placid pools make a liquid looking-glass for ash and birch, wild rose and hazel and yew, might be the home of the nymphs; and in that mossy vista, Adonis might find a couch of leaves:

And visions, as poetic eyes avow,
Hang on each leaf, and cling to every bough.

The silence of the wood carries with it a strange solemnity. A blue butterfly, like a winged flower, flits in the flickering light of the leaf shadows; once we catch sight of the disappearing brush of a squirrel; a field mouse is carrying food to its house in the ground; now and again a timid rabbit has stared at us and shown his little white tail. But the only sounds are the murmur of the river, the song of the grasshopper, and the rustle of leaves. The birds are speechless. There is the flutter of wings, but not the thrill of a feathered throat. In Spring when all the birds are either courting, or commencing housekeeping, the woods are noisy with their incessant opera; but now the eloquence of silence is well-nigh pathetic. Stay! a lonely robin has started a few plaintive notes. But there is no response to his pensive appeal. We are accosted by the contrasts in trees in which Nature delights. Here is a gnarled patriarchal oak, attended by a light winsome birch, which stands supple and beautiful at its side. It is a picture of age and youth, the one radiant hopeful and fair, the other seamed and scarred and furrowed by care and time. Close by the knotted trunk of this old oak, a little plant of green oak leaves is springing up where an acorn has taken root, and the parent tree stretches out its tottering paralysed arms as if to bless its posterity. More gnarled oaks and graceful silvery birches, as we climb the wooded path, fringed by fading bracken and spreading burdocks, and carpeted with fir-needles.

And now, behold! the Castle Rocks come abruptly in view; a fortress by Nature of black millstone grit embattlement projecting over the valley. At the foot of this bastion a tumult of loose rocks is strewn about like the *debris* made by a bygone bombardment. The view from the Pisgah summit of this Castle Cliff in the crisp slanting September light is one that photographs itself on the memory of both of us, and time will not readily efface the impression on the *camera lucida*. But it is difficult to convey the colour and contour of the picture in words. Perhaps the easiest way to deal with the task were to glibly dismiss the scene as difficult to imagine and impossible to describe, a method which is the favourite resort of ready writers. Yet it is very conventional scenery that the pen can reproduce, and it would be paying the present landscape but scant respect to leave out description altogether because of the difficulty of the performance. Better, I take it, an inadequate description to none at all. Even a few blurred lines, and badly mixed colours may assist the imagination more than utter blankness. Dip I, then, the 'prentice brush in the imperfect palette. The dark weather-worn Castle Rocks stand out from the wooded hill, and impend their pinnacles over a curve of deep valley at the bottom of which the Dane shines amid a dense green lining of spruce

B

and larch. Beyond the gleam of water and the gloom of wood in the valley, the hills spread for miles, wild tracts of bronzed heath under the wide sphere of uninterrupted sky, here and there broken by a bright patch of emerald pasturage, washed a cleaner green by recent rains, with white farmsteads standing out against bleak, blue-black pines, such as Turner loved to introduce in the shading of his pictures. Some of these isolated buildings are sheltered in the dip of moorland valleys; others are perched like eyries on the brow of hills right against the distant sky-line, with the sun flashing heliostate signals from their narrow window panes. All around is the fascination of great breadths of undulating space, and the spell of sunlit silence. To-morrow the whole sharp clear picture may be sponged out by the grey soaking mists that brood over these hills and blot out every outline.

And here the operations of the mental photographer are interrupted by a presence in an M.B. waistcoat, and with a copy of *Romola* under its arm, and a pensile appendage hanging below its clerical coat. (Doctor Molloy, of Dub. Unv., we greet you!) The tail was, ye disciples of Darwin, only a geological hammer, or rather a fishing-rod for catching fish of the ganoid and placoid genus that the sea left in shoals on the tops of the loftiest of these hills before the time of the first Navigator, Noah himself. The apparition is asking "Kalmat" the bearings of Ludchurch, which he cannot find. No wonder that he has missed it. Ninety-nine explorers in a hundred would miss it. Ludchurch is close by. A narrow cleft in the wooded hill-side is the doorway. It leads to a flight of rough-hewn steps of slippery stone. We descend. The riven rock, fern-covered and lichen-stained, rises on either side of us a sheer precipice. The Church is really a gorge in the gritstone, some 200 yards in length, several yards in width, some 40 feet in depth, and with a narrow entrance at either end. Young ash-trees and hazels form a roof of luminous green, rare plants and ferns and dwarf trees spring from every cleft; cool mosses robe the naked rocks; high up in a hazardous interstice a hawk has built its nest. At the further end of the Church a narrow slanting fissure opens out into an inner cavern ending in a perpendicular abyss which the most daring have not penetrated. Luckily the guide-book writers are ignorant of Ludchurch, and excursionists are unable to find it. For the sacred temple would be violated by the fern-gatherers and botanists, who ruthlessly tear out the leaves from the great, green, God-written Book of Nature, and who kidnap sweet ferns and flowers, lichens and mosses, and carry them away into captivity to pine away, pale prisoners, far from the nourishing influences, the dews and wind and shade and sweet air of their native hills.

There is something ineffably solemn about this romantic ravine. A lovable little friend of mine once asked when she was here during a passing thunderstorm: "Father, is this the place where God makes the thunder?" Sterner minds might almost endorse her tender fancy. This divine defile is linked with legend and history. Here Robin Hood, and his gigantic Little John, and his Sherwood outlaws, met to receive the benediction of their "curtal Friar." The persecuted Lollards, hunted down by the blood-hounds of persecution, sought refuge in Ludchurch, consecrating it by prayer and praise, sermon and psalm, and even baptizing its walls with their blood. Sir John Gilbert might seek inspiration for a pathetic picture in an incident of that troubled time. Here are the outlines. Walter De Lud-auk, the grey-haired Apostle of the proscribed Wickliffites, leading the simple devotions of his fervent followers. Close by him, his grand-daughter Alice, with her sylph-like figure, her streaming hair, her sweet face, her dulcet voice. She stands like May at the side of December, a picture of opening summer and declining winter. The fierce soldiers of Henry V. bursting, without warning, upon the sequestrated worshippers. The beautiful Alice lying killed in the assault by a shot from an arquebus, just when her escape is being made good by one of the Lollards, her lover, one Henrick Montair, a sturdy forester, equipped with crossbow and broad sword. Or an historical painter might find a picturesque subject in a more modern grouping of which Ludchurch was the scene, when the Pretender and his Highlanders camped in the ravine on their ill-starred march to Derby in the winter of '45, with Flora Macdonald, whose ringlets steal from under a slouching military hat, as she nurses her heroic hopes on the very spot where the December wind wails a requiem over the dust of Alice De Lud-Auk.

Ludchurch at its extreme end leads up an ascent of rugged steps out on to the open moor. We are above the Back Forest now. The entrance to its sylvan chapel is like a mouse-hole in a wall of green. Wide is the horizon from this wind-swept height. On one side the moors of Derbyshire and Cheshire stretch in bleak hungry solitudes with intersecting walls of grey-stone; while lo! on the other side reposes a vision of smiling farmsteads, and level meadows, and green hedgerows. And that sunny dream is Staffordshire. It is a striking scenic contrast. In front, a wild Scotch picture, up in the land of Lorne somewhere, behind a fair gentle English landscape. And fancy that soft, beautiful country side belonging to Staffordshire, noxious name, suggesting Acherontic streams of black poison, Cimmerian skies, hills of slag, valleys of coal-washings, people of pottery, home of Vulcan! A few miles away in the sunny haze is Congleton, with Congleton Car intervening, a burly peak, to block man's approach nearer the moors. Down there we can see the factory windows of unlovely Leek. They are only four or five miles away. But we are in a world of moor. The only sound is the call of a cock grouse. The heather gives under foot like a spring board. To the right rise the Roches. We take a shepherd's path across these cromlech-like crags. Once a sunburnt man in velveteens and gaiters, with gun and dog, takes a pipe of tobacco with us. He is a keeper. Grouse, partridges, and pheasants are to him the whole of existence. The 12th of August, and the 1st of September, and the 1st of October are the only anniversaries he wots of.

And so we tramp on through bog and bracken and bilberry, and the ever present purple heather bloom, 1,600 feet above the sea. The plover decoys us from its nest; ever and anon grouse rise strong on the wing in front. Three miles in length, the Roches are some two miles in breadth. The course lies from end to end of the rugged ridge, and our progress is inspired by " the live translucent bath of air," as vitalizing as the elusive Elixir of Life, which has been the search of the ages. Very bold and romantic is the scenery, almost unknown to painters. A quaint shrewd book published a century and a half ago, says:—" Here are vast rocks which surprise with " admiration, called the Henclouds and Leek Roaches. " They are so great a height, and afford such stupend- " ous prospects, that one could hardly believe that " they were anywhere to be found but in picture. " They are so bare that they have no turf upon them, " nor indeed any earth to produce it ; which whether " they were so from the Creation, or were uncovered " by the general Flood, or were washed clean by rain, " is not possible to account for." Our walk along this ridge is a romance in rock. Black, sepulchral, and uncanny rise the rugged millstone-grit crags above the broad undulations of heather. They assume strange shapes. Now a massive block, tapering at the end, and poised over a plateau, suggests a great breech-loader pointed at some far-off threatening mountain fort. Another stands an inscrutable eternal Presence, a sphinx indifferent to time, and unchanged by Age, a melancholy Menhir, silent, awful, with the secret of a pre-historic crisis hidden beneath its scarred, storm-rent breast. Other rocks, like colossal dragons, and petrified lions ; and still others, weather worn and wrinkled, which remind one of monsters of antediluvian birth, with grotesque heads, turned-up noses, blinking eyes, and mouths leering horridly. Here is a rocking stone; there a large-sized dolmen. And then, behold! at the summit of this ridge, close by where the sappers and miners have raised their flagstaff cairn, is a lonely, rush-fringed tarn, whose peat-coloured water catches the sunlight like a shield of steel. Still we have the awful cataclysm of crags around us, scattered like the brooding monuments of a dead world, the Necropolis of fabled giants. They are in two distinct lines now. One upright on a higher ridge; the other prostrate on a lower plateau that shelves abruptly into the valley. On the crags are shoals of fossil fish; underneath seams of coal and ironstone. I merely mention the fact as a curiosity. For neither of us regard the country with the mercenary manufacturing eye of the Philistines to whom the map of England is a geological chart representing coal measures and iron ore, and who look upon Cornwall as a tin mine, and North Wales as a big slate quarry, and the white crags of Derbyshire as containing so many cubic yards of pure limestone.

A little further on and a bridle-path, breast-high in bracken, leads us to Rock Hall, where there is another curious dolmen. Be not deceived by the appellation 'hall.' It is not the synonym in this instance for an ample country-seat and architectural stateliness. Rock **Hall is** simply a bleak keeper's lodge beneath the beetling cliffs. It belongs to Squire Brocklehurst, the owner of the Swythamley estate. **There** are antlers over the door, and black **old** oak within. Part of the retreat is a natural cave **made** cosy with furniture **that shines** like a smile. Another room is stone-built. **We are** welcomed to Rock Hall by a country-woman with broad dialect and apple-like face, streaked with red, like a Normandy pippin. She wears a tall snowy cap that makes her resemble **a Breton** peasant. **Did she** often see visitors? Oh yes, she had received Royalty, for had not the Prince and Princess Teck taken tea with her when their Highnesses were shooting **in this** neighbourhood? This comforting fact compensates the old lady for years of solitude. We have milk and **sweet** brown-bread **and** butter here, which is as acceptable to our freshened appetite as the most toothsome dishes ever packed in one of Fortnum **and** Mason's hampers. We rest and talk. It is pleasant to listen **to the** shrewd Mrs. Poyser-like sayings of this quaint dame, when lo! an **earnest** clock in an upright **oak case,** which **has** no doubt been wound up regularly **at a** certain time every Saturday night for ever so many years, startles us with a solemn warning, and then strikes the hour of five with a throbbing heart. It cannot be five o'clock? Impossible. But the faithful old clock always tells the truth, and would never be the means of one losing one's train and temper, if there were trains and tempers in these parts, bless you. And our watches point to five unmistakably. Conclusive confirmation is afforded to the very minute by a mouldering sun-dial at the door. Now, it will be remembered, that we left the ponies at half-past ten, and the coachman was instructed to wait four hours for us at the Royal Cottage. But the R. C. is yet several miles away. So we slide down the slope, and into the valley, gaining the road which leads us to an old-world village called Upper Hulme. A mill, and a church, and clustering houses are all mixed up among apple trees. A mountain brook, that washes over the pebbles, runs across the main road, where there is a ford for those who ride, and a mossy timber foot bridge for those who walk. And here there is an inn. The R. C. is some distance off yet; the refection of bread and butter and milk was ample enough in its way; but our tramp has been a long one, and again our vagus nerves are eloquent of that vacuum which nature abhors, and like Oliver, they ask for "more." So we decide to let the coachman linger longer. The order is ham and eggs and tea, and as we sit in the inn's best parlour, we can hear the sweet music of the ham hissing three or four rooms off, and ever and anon there steals upon us a savoury breath of its saline **flavour**.

Whilst we were soothing the vagus nerve, however, the best effects of the sunset were being wasted upon us. But there **is** still **a glory** in the west; **the** hills stand out in sharp outline against the low horizontal light; delicate tints soften the rocks. The light lingers long and lovingly **on** the silent hills, that seem to rest on the earth like rounded clouds, **as if loth to leave them to the** desolation of darkness. The intensity of the sunset glow has gone. There **are** black indigos and cold violets where there has been **a** flame **of** crimson **and** gold; but in the west there is a faint rose-red flush of fading colour, with a soft saffron spreading **to the** clouds above. The Hen Clouds and Lady Rocks, at the extremity of the Roches, stand out a black silhouette against the sky. They assume strange weird forms in the half-light of the darkening distance. There are still the ghostly bastions with great breechloaders about to open fire, and behind them are stony sentinels, who seem to wear long grey coats. Now they stand like picket-posts; anon bend stealthily over their guns. On one side of us is a deep mysterious wood; on the other the moors, which are now a picture in Indian ink. An owl with white silent wings wafts over us; once a hawk swoops hissingly down into the wood; a cock pheasant's plumage is seen against the white bark of a birch tree; a glow-worm shines like a fallen star. The flutter of a bat, the rustle of a rabbit, and the plaintive appeal of a peewit, make the silence intense. Almost imperceptibly the King of Day has died, and the pale Queen of Night, with her retinue of stars, begins her reign in the south. At first the stars show faint and far, but when the Royal Cottage is reached they are hanging low and lustrous.

Here we make the horrible discovery that our coachman, whom we expected was waiting to take us up, departed about an hour ago. "'E gotten tired o' weetin', and 'ee happen tho't ee'd mista'en 'is d'rections," is vouched in explanation. The Royal Cottage is a lonely hostelry that seems to have strayed among the moors, a hermit from habitations. Under its rafters Charles I. is said to have hidden—a hunted fugitive. But just at this moment we would rather the house possessed an available horse and trap than its historic reputation. "Quite a dash of adventure added to the day," says "Kalmat," carelessly, lighting his pipe, and we step out sturdily under the stars to Flash, where, perchance, our belated driver may be awaiting our arrival. There is nothing but moor on either side of us. The road is cut through it. The heather grows to its very verge. Ever and anon stone posts show at the edge of the intersecting road. They are placed there to mark the way for travellers in snow time. We seem to be on the top of the world. There is nothing between us and the sky, a wide perfect sphere of light. The stars seem near us. We have never seen so many of them before, not even in mid-ocean. There is something in the broad silence of the moors—black save where a peaty pool shines spectral and wan in the white moonlight; something in the awful expanse of the sky; something in the calm scrutiny of the stars which lifts the mind from the sentimental to the spiritual, and fills the soul with tender hopes, with higher aims, with a sense of the Infinite, with secret yearnings after what Browning calls "The Grand Perhaps." This feeling is accentuated as the wind wafts the sound of a hymn to us from a lonely little cottage of grey stone, far away from any signs of houses, with the yellow light from its windows thrown athwart the road. We pause in the reflection. There is a little gathering of week-night worshippers. A wheezy harmonium leads a few earnest singers; then an uncouth preacher with rough ringing voice who might be Adam Bede, prays from the heart for the weary and heavy-laden.

It was Charlotte Brontë who said that people had no conception of what a companion the sky becomes to anyone living in solitude—more than any inanimate object on earth, more than the moors themselves. It is so. The pole-star hanging like a lamp in front of us in the north, speaks to us like a friend; we become familiar with Charles' Wain, with Dick the plough-boy riding on the middle horse of 'the team; the far-off filmy milky way, spreading from north to south, grows palpable to our gaze. The brightest star is Mars, throbbing with a ruddy glow in the southeast. This session with the stars, is, perhaps, the tenderest sensation of the day; but it is not without satisfaction that we see the twinkling lights of the cottages at Flash, each telling a little tale of homely joy; and with something like hope we push to the inn. We find that our charioteer had enquired for us, waited, and left for Buxton. There is no accessible conveyance at Flash, and we have six miles more walking before us. So Shanks' pony is spurred on again with a disregard for the staying powers of that steed which calls for the merciful interference of the Society for the Prevention of Cruelty to Animals.

When we are taking the road along the lower slopes of Axe Edge, there is the distant sound of hoofs. Presently there is the gleam of carriage lights. We shout. The voice that responds is the glad cry of delight from Someone we both know well. She has been so put out at our absence. The coachman had been to St. Ann's and asked if we had returned. He thought that he had blundered over his intructions. And then the stupid man had caused the anxious heart to beat faster by a sinister suggestion that one of us might have fallen down the rocks. And so Our Lady had started out with the driver, a midnight Stanley, in search of the Livingstone of her heart. The rescuing party were equipped for this forlorn hope with Oscar, who comes to us with his cold nose and wagging tail, and with them they had a lantern, and a bottle of cognac. One of the tired tramps, in a spirit of very forced gaiety, says he would prefer to finish the journey on foot, but he is very glad to ride, and the demands made by his vagus nerve upon the supper would have shocked the medical world.

* * * * * *

All that we brought back with us was a sprig of heather. Its purple bloom is dried and faded now; but that little bit of moor carries with it an undying aroma of a rare, bright, happy, careless day; and it sometimes sends us back on the rough highway of memory to linger by one of the pleasantest landmarks in life's chequered journey.

THE
VALLEY OF THE GOYT.

Hie to haunts right seldom seen,
Lovely, lonesome, cool, and green.
SCOTT.

It all came about through Somebody—a sweet symphony in seal-skin—losing a skate-strap. The discovery of the loss—as paradoxical an expression by the way, as the "If I am found, then I am lost!" ejaculation of the hunted fugitive in the melo-drama—was made when we were approaching the Reservoir that supplies the Engine House on the High Peak Railway at Bunsal Cob. We had walked from Buxton along the Manchester Road—a distance of three miles—with the intention of cutting our initials on the ice.

"Have you ever seen the Goyt Valley in the depth of winter?" asked this bonny lithe maiden, the keen air heightening the beauty of her face with an unwonted colour.

"I have not even seen the Valley in summer," I was fain to confess, ashamed of my own ignorance.

"Then you shall make its acquaintance this afternoon," she said with a matronly air of decision. "It is an old and favourite friend of mine, and if you don't thank me for giving you an introduction, I will ——" But no matter. The threat was an idle one, and we chatted away merrily. We did'nt say anything clever, or poetical, or æsthetic; we posed in no attitudes of romantic admiration; and I am apprehensive that if our careless talk came to be coldly analysed it would be proved great rubbish. But the happiness of life, my friend, is not made up of heroics. It consists largely of little things; it is composed of trifles. And that afternoon we were both as happy as I daresay we ever shall be in this mundane sphere. But to return to that bright time.

It is a beautiful day at the end of November. That misanthropical month, so associated with drizzle and fog, has at Buxton redeemed its bad character by giving us a bright blue sky, and a thin clear crisp air that must be very trying to the able-bodied poor, since it trebles one's appetite, and gives the *genus homo* a whole series of antidyspeptic stomachs. Why Buxton is not replete with visitors is to me one of those puzzling phenomena

C

which, in the phrase of my Lord Dundreary, "no fellah can understand." Buxton in mid-winter is every whit as charming as Buxton in the height of the summer season. At a time when London and Manchester are choking with fogs that might be blasted with dynamite,—Buxton—a thousand feet above the mud and mist—has an elastic, lucent air that braces the nerves; and when the perverse east wind is making everybody peevish, the residents of this Derbyshire Spa are barricaded at every approach by barriers of determined hills from the assaults of the bronchitis-dealing blast; while the scenery of the Peak in winter has charms of which few people have any conception. For that matter, nature is as beautiful in her winter appearance as in her summer aspect. It seems so to my eyes, and Somebody emphasises my opinion with her endorsement. Of course the charm is a different one. It is as distinct in colouring and contour as the sunny light diaphanous muslin of Somebody in July, with bright flowers jewelling bosom and hat, is from the soft dark furs of that vivacious young lady in January. But there is a charm, nevertheless, just as there is one glory of the sun, another of the moon, and another of the stars. The picturesque side of winter has been neglected by painters. They represent Nature in Art only as seen six months out of the twelve. Then out-door landscape painting is a more luxurious occupation. In literary description the same one-sided practice largely prevails. Somebody protests that nearly all the pen-pictures of Derbyshire scenery which she has read have commenced: "It was a bright June morning;" or "The time was the merrie month of May;" or "The fair scene lay in the languid sunshine of sultry July."

"As if," she said, "there was no beauty about hills and valleys, no attraction in the moorland steppes, no grandeur in the tempestuous sunsets and twilights and cloud shadows of winter. As if men were so many dormice, and hibernated through the artistic winter months, when there is a sharpness of outline and a tenderness of colour on the hills, and a fresh elasticity in the air, which are lost in the heat and haze of summer."

All this she argued with an earnestness that became really eloquent by its manner, by the witching animation of eye and the musical inflexion of voice denied masculine orators from Demosthenes to Victor Hugo.

And yet Buxton is empty. The stray visitor monopolises the whole of the light, bouyant air of the place. Standing in the shadow of the Crescent, he is as much alone as if he were in the vast solitudes of Sahara, and he feels like a second-hand Marius, contemplating the desolation of a fashionable Carthage. The proprietors of the hotels are dining with each other to make up a table for dinner. They would, I verily believe, bribe a visitor just now for the curiosity of his patronage, unless in the process of treaty, the said visitor shared the fate of Actæon, and had his *disjecta membra* strewn along the Colonnade by competitive waiters tearing him in pieces in jealous rivalry. Some day, some celebrated person will suddenly discover what a delightful winter residence Buxton really is, just as Lord Brougham made Cannes by believing that that place agreed with him. Then it will become fashionable to repair to Buxton from October to March, and lodgings will be at a premium.

Me! Where, and oh where, have I left the reader during the digression? Pardon the long aside. Here we are regarding the skaters on the little lonely tarn among the moors, and picturesque enough is the scene. The atmosphere has the rich softness of a Claude landscape. There is such a golden mellowness in the November sunshine that the afternoon seems to swim under the lemon sky; across the ice, virgin white, save where some frozen-out labourers have swept broad black rings for skating, the westering sun, a ruddy copper shield, shines with a red horizontal light across wild tracts of hilly moors, with just a suggestion of snow relieving their sombre shade. There are great hollows in the moors, and there is an intersecting space between the hills which tells of a deep valley. Not a tree. Not a house. The only other object in the landscape, from the point whence our mental camera now focuses it, is the tall chimney of the solitary engine house of the High Peak Railway, a mineral line whose rails wind round miraculous curves and up extravagant gradients through Undiscovered Derbyshire, from Whatstandwell to Whaley Bridge. But the foreground of the picture is filled with a merry-moving steel-shod multitude, mostly Buxton residents, all mixed up in kaleidoscopic combinations, the patches of cardinal about the hats and throats of the girls, giving just the warm tints which a painter would distribute in the grouping. The captivating swing of that tall lissome lass now swiftly curving yonder, with the sun glancing on the blades of her skates, is one of the most graceful sights possible; for a handsome English maiden skating makes really a fine picture, as stately as the pose of a swan, or the movement of a yacht. Somebody is delighted with two bright-eyed girlettes —vignettes in black velvet and clocked stockings— who are being taken in tow across the ice by a big

St. Bernard dog, and it would be difficult to say which most enjoys the fun: the harnessed animal or the two bonnie weans. That is their brother learning to strike out, and tumbling down very often. But, bless you, he never seems satisfied with the frequency of his falls, and is adding to their number, when Somebody, nudging my elbow, says:

"We are not stationary engines, and I must really remind you that our exploration will involve some walking."

Without being tediously topographical, I may remark that the valley of the Goyt is approached from Bunsall by a road called Goyts Lane. A rough declivitous road, more like the dry bed of a bygone mountain torrent, than the carriage way it claims to represent. Heath, cranberry, bilberry, and wortleberry infringe on either side, and sometimes dispute the possession of the road with the traveller altogether. The bilberry leaves are a vivid green among the prevailing neutral tints.

Presently comes a glimpse of firs and larches, pine and spruce, on the bank rising out of the valley, and now behold! there is Goyts Bridge: a wooded hollow amid the meeting of waters. There is a grey farmhouse, and here and there the blue film rises from a cottage mixed up in dark patches of pine and fir. A solitary arch of lichened stone spans the little voiceful river, which rising from the slopes of Axe Edge—the great water shed of the Peak District—dissects Cheshire and Derbyshire, even as the Dove and the Dane, running in different directions, divide Derbyshire and Staffordshire, and flowing in a deep channel by New Mills is robbed of its sweet music by money-making manufacturers, who blacken its pure, transparent life, until sick, and sluggish, and impure, it crawls feebly into the Mersey near Stockport.

"Why"—asks Somebody in an indignant and injured manner—"why do we hold guiltless the greedy gold-grasping men who poison our beautiful streamlets? For private gain they disfigure the very face of God Himself, and stifle the voice of His Spirit."

I must talk seriously to Somebody about Political Economy.

At Goyts Bridge, the road to the right leads to Errwood Hall, to which Somebody is wishful to take her charge another day. Our present path is that to the left, and follows up the river as it runs away from its mountain home. The spot is musical with the meeting of waters. A grey stone arch spans a tinkling tributary; there is an old cottage, with an interior like a bit of Tenier's; together with a picturesque blending of swift water, projecting rock, and hanging tree, that might be a scene specially "set" by Nature for a stage-picture.

There is not in the wide world a valley so sweet,
As that vale in whose bosom the bright waters meet;
Oh! the last rays of feeling and life must depart,
Ere the bloom of that valley shall fade from my heart.

So carols Somebody, who has already forgotten all about the millocracy of New Mills and Stockport. For we are now in the deep canon, pursuing a narrow path that rises and falls and skirts small precipices. And which of us will first forget that sudden vision of a long vista of valley, seen under a cold lemon sky, with the eager voiceful river breaking over a tumult of mossy boulders in a thousand white waterfalls, and here and there catching a tinge of red from the frosty sun? At the bank-sides, where the current is not swift, the water is frozen, and little tributary water-threads have a surface of thin clear ice under which we see the water moving like quicksilver. There are icicles on the grey lichened rocks, and crystals of snow shine on the roadway, which winds high above the torrent. The dark-limbed trees are brought out in sharp relief by the white rime of hoar-frost, feathery, fantastic, lace-like; and the needles of the firs are coated with shining crystals. But the light covering of rime and snow cannot hide the carpet of faded oak, and copper beech, and broad Spanish chestnut leaves, which lie ankle deep in heaps of red and brown and yellow. There is scarcely any foliage left on those trees, but on either bank soldierly rows of dark green fir and pine and larch are drawn up in line to salute the river as it passes in hasty review. On the hazel are threads of scarlet; a few red haws remain on the hawthorn; and there is the plumlike bloom of the black sloe. But for the ceaseless song of the river—now soft and tender in a minor key, like a lover's entreating whisper; now a sweet lullaby, with a note of sadness in it, sung to the silent and listening rocks, as the water reposes in contemplative pools that mirror bits of sky; then a gay careless shout, a loud defiant laugh, as it wakens from its reflective mood and dashes in restless madcap race heedlessly past lichened rocks and stretched-out arms of compassionate trees that try to stop its flight;—but for this voiceful water, I say, absolute silence would reign in the valley. Frost and snow hold Nature in quiet restraint. We have seen, it is true, the robin and the tom-tit; once there has come the sceap-sceap of a snipe, rising in zig-zag flight, with breast as brown as the fallen chestnut leaves; once the missel-thrush has shown his spotted chest; once we have caught sight of the golden bill of the blackbird. There are the footprints of rabbits and hares; we hear the hollow note of the wood-pigeon; and Somebody says that she has seen the heron sitting watchful and weird by the water when the gloom has been gathering in this wild solitude.

As we pass up the valley the walk increases in its lonely beauty. At Goyts Clough, where a torrent roars across the path, the rocky sandstone sides of the stream break suddenly into moorland escarpments, and these stretch into higher expanses of moorland, that rise and fall until their far-off waves meet the purple line of the horizon. And now the aspect of the valley is altered. The trees cease, the bronzed moors rise precipitously from the stony bed of the stream, and encompass it on either hand. Presently, to our right, are one or two houses that seem to make the solitude all the more lonely. The sun has insensibly gone down, and there is a metallic twilight. The glimmer of a candle shines in one of the ghostly cottage windows. Close by is an old gritstone quarry, which has a story that belongs to the romance of trade. It was first worked by the originator of parcel-vans, the Pickford whose name is as familiar to us as Her Majesty's face on pence and postage stamps. That was in the days of last century. The flagstones which paved the Regent-street of those days were hewn from this quarry. They were carted all the way to London, via Leek.

Brindley had not then developed his water-highways, and George Stephenson, in his pitman's clothes, was learning to read and write for fourpence a week at a night-school. But canals came to be made, and railways were constructed, and it became no longer profitable to pave Piccadilly from the Peak. The supply of stone in this quarry is by no means exhausted, but the cost of carriage renders its working no longer profitable. Time, which deals gently with most wounds, has healed the scars the quarrymen of a past generation inflicted on the cliff, and with lichen and ivy, fern and foliage and flowers, has lovingly repaired the ruin caused years ago.

And now we leave the river-side and strike across the moors. We are alone on the top of the world. The moon looks down upon us with pale steadfast gaze; the stars regard us with a thousand eyes. The road shows wan in the wide space of encompassing moor. A far-off group of gloomy pines stand ghost-like in the white light. The only sound is caused by the plaintive cry of that bird of triple name—lapwing, peewit, plover. Once, too, the curlew—"the Whaup" of William Black's "Daughter of Heth"—rises with its sharp wings in swift flight, with a shrill call with a roll in it, just like a pea-whistle. Far away in front is a yellow light from a solitary little farmhouse which has made a scanty clearing in the moor. Somebody is strangely silent. The cold refining light of the moon touches her face with a saintly radiance. And at last when she speaks there is an unwonted tremor in the soft voice. She says:—

"I sometimes think that to be in the middle of a moor under the stars is to experience more spiritual feeling than is induced in the solemnest cathedral or by the most earnest sermon."

It appears that she knows the people at the house whose yellow window, in the broad space of mysterious moor, shews like a lighthouse gleam in mid-ocean. An old woman, with a white mob-cap—something like what the fashionable ladies of æsthetic South Kensington are reviving to-day—sits in the ingle-nook smoking a clay pipe of marvellous colouring. There is a smell of peat about the fire; the only pictures on the walls are in the shape of substantial sides of bacon; there is a cheese knife on the table fashioned out of the old broad-sword of a cavalier. The ancient dame is crooning alone, "John"—the sharer of her years—"has gone to Booxton to pay th' rent to th' Duke," and she is fretful that he will be "coming whoam full up wi' yell which'll do his rheumatics a power o' harm." And she puffs away silently at the consoling pipe. And

Somebody, with a tender consideration for the weakness of old people, quietly prompts me to leave the whole contents of my own pouch to solace the old lady's hours. It is one of the aged dame's boasts that she has never slept out of that house for over fifty years. Half a century spent in vegetation. To the dwellers in busy towns, who crowd so much experience and so many sensations into each day, these isolated hill people do not seem to live. The number of their days is longer than ours, and the days are longer, but one day is so much like another, that their existence is only a monotonous routine of food and sleep, a slow process of going to the grave. They do not really feel the pulse of life.

> *They from to-day and from to-night*
> *Expected nothing more*
> *Than yesterday and yester night*
> *Had proffered them before.*

And yet, perhaps, these simple dull quiet people are happier in their lives than we, with our daily discontent and fever fret.

The moon shines on the waves of moorland in a long path of white light, just as it does on the sea, making, as it seems, a silver road upon which you might walk up to the entrance of Heaven. But what is that strange object in front of us standing out in sharp silhouette between moon and stars? It is a man, but his steps over the rough uneven way are very erratic. He is walking in figures of eight. The old lady in the lonely farm yonder was quite right in her sorrowful apprehensions. It is "John," and he is, indeed, "full up wi' yell." He is made more grotesque by a number of parcels—for he has been shopping—which, he being unable to carry, are tied all over his body. We console with him about his rheumatics; and his efforts to balance himself in a dignified perpendicular position of attention are as broadly comic as a farce. "Oi munna stop and talk or Oi shall set," he says at last, and the honest old man stumbles on, paying his attentions to both sides of the road.

The path across the moor brings us on to the Macclesfield road just above Burbage, where we are a mile from Buxton, whose gas lamps in the hollow strike strange to eyes which have grown accustomed to the sharp lights and dark shadows of the moors. When we get back to the town, we have walked altogether about eight or nine miles. The exercise and the air have given us appetites that are Homeric in their greatness, and the old-fashioned knife-and-fork tea in the snugly-curtained room, with its glowing fire and wax candles, is not the least acceptable sensation of the day.

And afterwards Somebody is not too tired for music. And has she, perhaps, a lingering vision in her memory of that deep, still, beautiful, secluded valley of the afternoon, where a dozen rivulets and rills join their young voices in a perpetual hymn, which only the bending trees and the grand old hills are privileged to hear, when she sings;

Sweet vale of Avoca! how calm could I rest
In thy bosom of shade, with the friends I love best,
Where the storms that we feel in this cold world should cease,
And our hearts, like thy waters, be mingled in peace.

CLIMBING COMBS MOSS.

Will you go with me to the moors?
To the land of grouse and heather—
Yon level ridge in the distance,
Where hill and sky meet together?
One hour from where we are standing,
In sound of the forge and the hammer,
And you'll hear the crow of the moor cock,
And the lapwing's ceaseless clamour.

J. H. J.

A January morning at Buxton. Grey sky, gusty east wind, and grim black frost. There is a friendly glow in the fire; across the room the cold window frames a picture of sullen hills drawn in Indian Ink. The North-Easter has lost its temper, and is shrieking because no one ventures out to do battle with its vengeance.

"Just the morning for a ten mile walk as a tonic before dinner!" says the Young Man breaking in upon some touch-and-go criticism of the poetry of *Festus*, which I am enjoying with Somebody, with frank grey eyes and good-natured mouth. She has got Philip James Bailey's volume, a gift of the poet, resting in her lap. By the way, who reads *Festus* now? a dramatic poem of which Alfred Tennyson said that he "could scarcely trust himself to say how much he admired it, for fear of falling into extravagance." It is a remarkable composition, and all the more remarkable because its author was barely three and twenty when it was given to the world. But he has never done anything of merit since this youthful masterpiece. He exhausted himself for all time.

> *He sang himself hoarse to the stars very early,*
> *And cracked a weak voice to too lofty a tune.*

Single Speech Hamilton; One Book Bailey. I think his Muse obtained a pecuniary recognition from Government. Perhaps if he had received no pension we should have had more poetry.

But to return to the Young Man. He is not thus called because he is young, for his beard has long been iron-grey, and the steel ploughshare of Time has left deep furrows in the fine-featured face; but because his heart is full of juvenility and his sympathies are all with youth. One of us, indeed, proposed to dub him "The Boy." He takes a school-lad's fresh interest in country-life, and his greatest delight is to romp with children, or pause

D

to have a *tête à tête* with little strangers of the mature age of five and six, whom he may casually encounter in his travels. I should not be astonished to find him setting a back at leap-frog, or playing at shuttlecock and battledore, when he is eighty. Although he is now in his sixth decade, and is surely old enough to know better, he has been exposed to the genteel disgust of his grown-up family "knuckling down" at ring-taw with the small urchins of the neighbourhood; and only last spring he went bird-nesting with some young lads, finding the mossy nests for them, but, mark you, not permitting the theft of a single egg, or fledgling, for the Young Man is as much a champion of wild birds as St. Francis D'Assisi was a friend of fishes. When remonstrated with by an indignant potentate in petticoats, he quotes a favourite author to prove that cricket has been made a manly game simply that men may think themselves boys for an hour or two.

The Young Man, in addition to these dreadful deformities of character, is the only person in the world I ever found to agree with the Rev. Charles Kingsley's love for the north east wind. "To be able to enjoy the brave east wind is a sure sign of good health, my nephew," he says, after he has dragged me away from the genial fire, and the warm grey eyes, to face the gloomy Hyperborean hills.

> *Welcome, black North-Easter!*
> *O'er the German foam;*
> *O'er the Danish moorlands,*
> *From thy frozen home.*
>
> . . . , . . .
>
> ***Jovial*** *wind of Winter,*
> ***Turn us out*** *to play!*
> ***Sweep the*** *golden reed-beds,*
> *Crisp the lazy dyke;*
> *Hanger into madness*
> *Every plunging pike.*
> *Fill the lake with wild fowl·*
> *Fill the* ***marsh*** *with snipe;*
> *While on dreary moorlands*
> *Lonely curlews pipe.*
> *Through the black fir-forest,*
> *Thunder harsh and dry,*
> *Shattering down the snow-flakes*
> *Off the curdled sky.*
>
> . . . .
>
> *Come, and strong* ***within*** *us*
> *Stir the Vikings' blood;*
> *Bracing brain and sinew,*
> *Blow, thou wind of God!*

These are the lines the athletic sexagenarian is singing as I **pull** on my gloves and button up my coat, and Somebody is very solicitous about a certain warm woollen comforter, almost as big as a blanket.

Once outside, there is something strong and healthful in the dash of cold air that inspires courage; and the ramble we have before us is through a wild track of picturesque country **that** is new to me, and one which my friend's ecstatic descriptions have led me, in the drudgery of a dull life in a dingy office, to look forward to with no ordinary anticipation. We are bound for Coombs Moss (from "Cwm," the Celtic for a curved piece of country, as in this instance). A romantic solitude upon whose heather the foot of the tourist has seldom trod. It is quite near Buxton, yet very far away from Buxton; and while artists would revel in its scenic charms, antiquarians would delight in its interesting historic relics: but practically the place has yet to be discovered. "I only know two English neighbourhoods thoroughly, and in each, within a circle of five miles, there is enough of interest and beauty to last any reasonable man his life. I believe this to be the case almost throughout the country." So wrote the author of "Tom Brown's School Days" in reference to the White Horse Vale, and the observation applies with special force to the Peak of Derbyshire.

The Young Man makes light work of the steep slopes of the Corbar Woods, in their winter aspect very different to the dense green forest which summer visitors haunt. Overhead there is now no fretwork roof of lambent foliage, through which the sunlight steals with a softened radiance; underfoot there is no tangled carpet of wild flowers. The bracken is brown; the ferns are yellow and sad. The pleasant summer glades of cool green are now represented by black trunks and bare, frosted branches. The incessant concert of birds is hushed. One misses, too, the sweet confusion of lovers whose reverie has been disturbed by encroaching footsteps. The only sound is the axe of the woodman. The woods are being thinned by the Duke's forester, for the growth has become too thick. Several trunks lie athwart the path, others still standing bear the fatal white paint cross of destruction. Among the winding walks, so cool and fragrant and beautiful a few months ago; across the secluded bridge where Mr. Manchester has so often plighted his troth with Miss Liverpool, and Miss Birmingham, with the deadly eyes, made promises to Mr. Sheffield, with pretty lips that have since perjured themselves, and with honeyed smiles that are now sweetening another's hours; still ascending the lovers' path, until the very summit of Corbar is reached. And now above stretches a vast expanse of moor. This is Coombs Moss, a mountain ridge several miles long and one or two miles across. We are to explore it this morning. Buxton lies below, shut completely in with barriers of hills. The town lies, as it were, at the bottom of a tea-cup. Across in the cold grey mist is the hill locally known as Solomon's Temple;

behind it the bladelike contour of **Axe Edge** stands
out clear and defined with waves of brooding mist
below it. The Young Man, to whom this grey peak
of the Midlands is as dear as the Matterhorn is to
an enthusiastic member of the Alpine Club, says he
has often clomb the hill when there has been a sea
of clouds beneath him, but a sky of vivid blue
above; and in winter he has stood on its summit
when a snow-storm has beat below, blotting out the
earth in a dancing mist of white, while the sun
blessed the head of the mountain with its beams,
and left it unspotted by the wintry element. Cawton
Hill and Chelmorton Low are high in cloudland;
yonder is Priestcliffe; there the hills encompassing
Tideswell; while that indistinct nebulous mass, dif-
ficult to decide whether it be mist or mountain, is
Mam Tor, the shivering mountain of Castleton.

We strike across the moor. The North-Easter at
this altitude shaves one like an atmospheric razor,
and, as Mr. Ruskin says of the oxygen-laden wind of
the Yorkshire wolds, "you can almost lean against
it." The long beard and moustache of the Young
Man are being frozen into matted iron; there is ice
on the mouthpiece of my pipe; but we perspire with
the plunging exercise through the springy heath
which we, being lovers of birds and loathers of the
battue, protest has all the glow and excitement of

grouse shooting without its cruelty. Several grouse rise, but at long distances from us. Once a hare starts from our feet. But there seems an utter suspension of life. The moors are a picture of wild desolation, and a cold loneliness, that is not altogether without poetic fascination. The black rigour of the frost seems to hold everything fast in its iron grip. The peaty pools are frozen; there is a great stillness; everything is dead; the prevailing colour is dead; a neutral tint, a shroud of swathing mist, a brooding cold grey that half hides and half reveals. The moors themselves seem to be a vast black sea of raging billows suddenly checked in the height of a storm and held in eternal arrest. The heather, regarded as a mass, is a dark bronzed green like velvet, and is as attractive to the artistic eye as in its wine-stained purple of full bloom. But taking the individual plant it is withered and dead. One looks in vain for a single sprig of green, and recalls the aching pathos of that passage in Mrs. Gaskell's Life of Charlotte Brontë, where the author of " Jane Eyre" went over the December moors searching in the little hidden hollows and sheltered nooks for a lingering spray of heather, just one spray—however withered—to take to her sister Emily, and found that the flower was not recognised by the filmy, fading eyes. Coombs Moss, indeed, is just such a moor as the strange wild-bird like nature of Emily Brontë loved, for here are the vast spaces, the sense of freedom and of loneliness, which gave to her dauntless poetic nature such ministering companionship. But if the heather is dead, the bilberry is a bright green, for it is freshest in the depths of winter, and duskiest in the summer; while in the protected clefts and sheltered crevices of the gritstone are beautiful lichens and mosses that are miracles of colour. The Young Man points out a bold rock that is called Robin Hood's Tor. It was the scene of one of the Sherwood hero's hunting exploits, when he———but no matter. The story is quite a mile long. At least we have got over that space of ground while the Young Man, a lover of legends, has been detailing the country-side tradition. We are now making our way across the moor to its north-eastern extremity to something less apocryphal: an actual Roman Camp, as complete as it was when the warriors of Julius Agricola left it.

Our steps are directed thither, the Young Man diminishing the distance with a fund of local anecdote that is as unfailing as the widow's cruse of oil. A grouse at last rises near us. It flies up almost at our feet with a startled cluck-cluck-cluck, and then alights a few yards off with a temerity which the Young Man cannot disturb. The bird is waiting for his timid wife, who is trembling somewhere near us and is afraid to join her lord and master. He accosts her impatiently, and now there is a sudden flutter of brown feathers as the dear lady has summoned up courage, and the wedded pair fly away into the misty distance, evidently under the delusion that the 12th of August has arrived prematurely. Our next acquaintance is a horned ram as black as his native millstone grit. We approach him, and he contemplates us with a grave stare of critical scrutiny. After he has judiciously summed us up, he gives vent to a bah! of unmistakable contempt, and walks off with an air of disdain in his curly horns, and lofty scorn in his dirty fleece, to tell his club of the strange creatures trespassing on his estate. The Young Man says that these mountain sheep are very different animals to your domesticated meadow mutton. They are as wild as the hills they range. Fierce and defiant, when a hostile dog is after them they will take the rough stone walls of the country like stags. And he also adds something about their superior culinary qualities. *Entre nous* a regard for *selle de mouton* is not one of the least of the Y. M.'s characteristics. But *revenons à nos moutons*, if the expression is not paradoxical when it is sheep that we have been discussing.

Presently, as we approach the eastward edge of the Moss, there comes a patch of blue in the cold, grey, gusty sky. The mists that have been trailing along the hills are lifting. The sun, as yet, does not absolutely shine; but his presence is indicated by a lance of yellow light that strikes athwart the Landseer mists of the landscape. And far below us is a deep broad vale shut in with bold hills whose burly shoulders claim attention by their aggressive attitude. Chapel-en-le-Frith hides down in the hollow; and lo! there is a broad mere which is not frozen, for the water shivers in the wind. The Young Man vouches that it is only the Chapel Reservoir; an artificial lake formed by a natural basin. But are we not in Wordsworth's country? Say, is not that Grasmere? The expanse of water certainly gives to this Derbyshire landscape a charm which Derbyshire landscapes emphatically lack. Who was it who said that a landscape without water is like the human face without the eye? And now behold! the sun with a sudden burst turns the drawing in Indian ink into a radiant water-colour picture. The light touches the water, and the silver spreads over the cold black surface until it is a damascened sheet of liquid light, framed in a setting of grey-green, where the irregular banks and grassy promontories, which give the water a picturesque variety, are reflected. The burnished expanse is broken only when a fitful gust of wind ruffles it in dark ripples. The day is fast brightening. Hills that have been invisible now sketch themselves in the picture with great clearness of outline. The Young Man enthusiastically proposes a vote of thanks to his Puissant Majesty, the Clerk of the Weather, for turning on the opportune sunshine; it is seconded by his companion-in-arms, supported by both, and carried unanimously. And now the views on every side have broadened to the vision, as if seen through a powerful telescope. Distant objects stand out sharp and clear in the thin bright air; the lake below mirrors a patch of blue sky. The little mist lingering in the valley is now a silver gauze. Taxall,—Lyme Moor,—Disley,—Whaley Moor,—Eccles Pike,.—Chinley Churn,—Dympus,—rattles off the Young Man pointing to this and that hill, with his stick, like the descriptive lecturer at a penny panorama. To our left, right across a vale in the north, are the sombre shoulders of Kinderscout, the highest point in Derbyshire; the isolated Peak on the opposite side to the right is Cracken Edge, on whose summit a famous landscape painter, in a notable picture, placed Joshua commanding the sun to stand still, while in the valley the warriors of Israel were vanquishing with great vigour the army of the

Amorites. Tom Moore conceived Lalla Rookh, with its gorgeous glow of scenery and vivid oriental colouring, by the bleak banks of the Dove; but it was even a greater geographical achievement to pass off this hungry Derbyshire hill as a peak in Palestine, and that Chapel-en-le-Frith dale as the valley of Ajalon.

The expansive view which we are now comprehending is the same as the soldiers of Cæsar beheld, as their sentries looked down upon the country and watched with strained eyes for the rising of any of the desperate, disaffected Britons whom the Roman legions had driven from the Derbyshire leadmines and lime-workings. Here at this northern termination of the Moss, at an elevation of 1670 feet above the sea-level, is the Roman fort. Look how clearly from the valley the artificial chariot-road, a ruled line of green amid the dark heath, climbs the stubborn side of the hill until it reaches a level plateau at the summit. This flat and angular platform is flanked with precipitous escarpments several hundred feet in height and invulnerable against attack; while on the southern boundary are formidable entrenchments still distinctly definable. The inspection of this ancient stronghold is like reading a chapter of history. The memory sees more than the eye, and the imagination peoples the silent trenches with helmeted men armed with shield and spear. The Young Man points out the fountain in the centre of the Camp. It quenched the thirst of valiant warriors dead these two thousand years, but the clear water is bubbling up still a perpetual spring, the emblem of immortal youth. We also stumble, when at the northern angle of this old-world fortress, upon excavations which are said to be the remains of cairns, or sentry shelters; and the Young Man has jotted down in his pocket book from Professor Sainter's "Scientific Rambles" the exact dimensions of the Camp. Here are the figures :—

	FEET.
Length of fosse and ramparts	547
Width of outer fosse at top of cutting	30
Depth of outer fosse from level of ground	10
Height of first or outer rampart from bottom of outer fosse	20
Width of inner fosse at top of ramparts	50 to 65
Depth of inner fosse from top of ditto	10
Height of inner rampart	10
Length of west side of camp	450
Length of north east side of camp	466
Length of entrance to camp, including path	366

The supreme idea of the Roman strategists, in entrenching this windy table-land, was to command an outlook over as large an area of country as possible. From this unassailable eyrie they had certainly one of the most expansive prospects in the Peak. At the foot of the fortress right down in the wide valley, may be seen in the summer days another encampment, for regiments of Her Majesty's infantry of the line, from the depots of Manchester or Sheffield, camp out here and have target practice in a country as wild as the defiles of Afghanistan or the dhongas of Zululand. And a very picturesque sight it is in the soft, hot, hazy weather to see the red-coats scattered over the heather, little patches of bright colour amid the bold inequalities of the hills, pinging away with the Martini-Henry under the very camp where the imperial eagle waved its symbol of conquest in days when the Nazarene was performing His miracles.

When the Romans left the country, and their Saxon successors lost it, Coombs Moss overlooked the Royal Forest of the Peak of Derbyshire. It was held by William Peverill, the illegitimate son of William of Normandy. Peak Forest is now a railway station, and the blasting of the limestone companies is heard where once the woodman's horn awoke responsive echoes. Chapel-en-le-Frith, according to the Young Man, owes its name to the fact of the foresters and keepers of the deer becoming so numerous that about 1225 they purchased a portion of the crown lands held by one William de Ferrers and erected for themselves a chapel for divine service, which they named the

Chapel in the Forest (firth). The ancient chapel is as dead as the sturdy green-woodsmen who built it, and the present church has neither the attraction of age nor architectural beauty to detain us.

Coombs Moss falls away rapidly into Dove Holes, for which place we make with appetites as sharp as any that may have belonged to Roman soldier or Norman forester. Dove Holes is the picturesque name for a commonplace lime-burning village which has a station on the North-Western system, while it gives a name to a long tunnel, perforating a massive hill, on the main line of the Midland to Manchester, between Peak Forest and Chapel-en-le-Frith. There was something big in landslips here some years ago; while the history of the tunnel is in itself a romance; a fascinating story of unyielding engineering skill conquering insurmountable forces. More than three years were spent in this difficult undertaking. Water-springs in the rock defied both capital and labour. At the present time there is an underground stream in this vault in which trout and grayling are so numerous that it has been suggested by a practical angler they should be captured and transferred to the over-fished waters of the Wye and Derwent. Fancy trout in a tunnel; imagine grayling in the gloom.

It is a sudden transition from the broad silence

and the sublimity of the moorland mountain to this commercial village of Dove Holes, with its public-houses, and its hulking "corner-men" at each turn of a street. There is a train bound for Buxton in a few minutes, and, leaving the Young Man to propitiate with a penny the shrill anguish of a little fellow, who has fallen down and broken a jug, I hasten to the rabbit-hutch of a booking-office to take tickets.

AN
EXCURSION TO ERRWOOD

The rooks scarcely swing **on the tops of the trees,**
While river-reeds nod to the tremulous **breeze;**
A rose-leaf, **a-bask in** *the sunshiny gleam,*
Half *sleeps* **in** *the dimples that chequer the stream;*
The dragon-fly hushes his day-dreamy lay,
The silver *trout sulks in his sedge-shaded bay.*

J. ASHBY-STERRY.

"Driver!"

The Buxton petrifaction does **not hear us,** and the horses crawl lazily up **a very** easy gradient. **When** the address is repeated, the man turns round on his box respectfully.

"We are not going **to** a funeral!" says the Young Man, cheerily.

There is no improvement in the sluggish **pace for** the moment. Then, quite suddenly, the Derbyshire Jehu breaks out into a spasm of wiry activity. He tugs the reins, brandishes the whip, shouts to the pair of horses, and away we go at a reasonable trot. The mortuary observation only took a minute or two to make its occult meaning clear, which is, indeed, a very short space of time for the average Peak intellect to receive and understand a joke. Sydney Smith, who must be credited with the few good things Shakespeare left unsaid, placed the assertion on record that it requires a surgical operation to get a joke into the head of a Scotchman; and it is said that at a supper-party, and in passing a plate, Theodore Hook made a madly-outrageous pun that convulsed with spontaneous merriment everybody in the room but one man, who did not even smile, but who, more than an hour afterwards, and to the surprise of all, abruptly broke out into the broadest of laughs and complimented the wag on the joke he had made over supper. That man was either Scotch or Derbyshire born. Misty hills must induce a mental melancholy that the sunshine shaft of wit takes time to pierce. Not that there was much of the sunshine shaft of wit in the remark we made to our charioteer. But even so transparent a joke took careful consideration.

May is merging into June, and we are bound for the Home of the Rhododendron: Errwood. Topographically I may be wrong in including Errwood in

Undiscovered Derbyshire. Really it is in Cheshire, but it only belongs to that county by the width of the little river Goyt. At any rate Errwood is in the Peake countrie, and only **a matter of four** or five miles from **Buxton.**

We **leave the carriage at the** Engine House at Bunsall Cob, better known as Long Hill, only having availed ourselves of the vehicular convenience because of the encumbrance of an easel and a fishing-rod; for Somebody is going to take a treasured beauty-spot back with her on canvas, and **the** Young Man proposes to try the fortunes of a new artificial fly in a deep pool in the Goyt, where plump trout lie lazily poising their speckled bodies under the shade of wooded banks. So the charioteer is dismissed with instructions to pick us up again at the same place at the close of the day.

Leave we artist and angler awhile to their amusements, while we stray round Errwood.

Instead of taking the turn to the left at Goyts Bridge, and following the road **up the** river, we pursue the road to the right. A walk of a hundred yards brings us to the lodge gates of Errwood. The carriage drive up to the Hall is before us. Be not deceived by the appellation carriage drive. Conjure up no decorous roadway of mathematically ruled gravel, dissecting methodically shaven grass. Im-

agine no stiff roadway as "county family" as the
severe Squire that owns it. There is nothing formal
about this carriage drive. It runs at the bottom of
a wild valley, where nature assumes one of her most
romantic moods. A blithe mountain stream sings
by its side all the way. Bold rocks and steep wooded
slopes shut it in on either hand. There is the shade
of foliage and of deep wooded ways everywhere.
Banks of hollies, with the red berries of winter still
glowing in the dark gloss of the green; pines and
firs of majestic height, very different to the bleak,
ragged, storm-shrivelled trees on the hills, trees
which turn to the East as if trained in strict Ritual-
istic observances; but Goliaths of their race, just
like the giant firs and pines that are the glory of the
Duke of Argyll's forest at Inverary, by the banks of
the brawling Aray and under the shadow of the peak
of Duniquoich. But it is not for these splendid
growths that Errwood is famous. Behold the pride
of the place! See the rhododendrons rising tier
above tier, tint upon tint. Pelian piled upon Ossa
a blaze of bloom. They are not plants; they are
trees. They rise in ramparts of flowers. It is an
artist's study of colour, these tints, from the deep
Tyrian imperial purple to faint blush of pink, with
every seeming gradation of rose-red, scarlet, vermil-
lion, lake, carnation, cardinal, and all relieved by the

deep glossy green of the dense leafage, toned down still more by the sombre foliage of fir and pine and yew. This is, indeed, the Home of the Rhododendron. Forty-thousand plants—according to the unimpeachable testimony of the Young Man—were set here some thirty years ago, and they have flourished into this magnificent growth.

The road winds uphill at the base of these towering walls of showy flower, and the little tributary stream hurries down under arches of foliage and ferns, cascading now with a shout of joy over a lichened rock; pausing now in a quiet cool pool where water plants bend low and kiss the sweet-faced water. There is a lark, a speck of thrilling song, in the June blue above; the wooded slopes of the deep green valley are full of unstranslatable melody; but surely the sweetest sound to be heard is the voice of that joyous streamlet, as it hugs the road all the way down the drive. A mountain rivulet, taking its tributary wave to the ocean, surely does make the sweetest music St. Cecilia can evoke; tenderer in the piannissimo passages, more exultant in the full forte, than the notes of a Malibran, a Lind, a Titians, a Patti.

Errwood Hall stands on a plateau commanding a view that would exhaust the ornate descriptive powers of a George Robins. The vision comprehends the whole of the deep green wooded valley, with a range of moorland heights beyond. The house is the home of the Grimshaws, a Roman Catholic family. The white stone mansion is in the Italian style, and a crucifix one sees at an upper window lends to the mind the delusion that the scene is Italian too:

*A deep vale
Shut out by Alpine hills from the rude world.*

On the summit of the hill above Errwood Hall—an observatory which gives an expansive panorama of rising and falling hill and moor—is the Mausoleum Chapel. At this height the wind comes with a cool caress to the face; there is the hum of the bee among the heather; a butterfly flies past like a winged flower. Down again by the Hall. We will return, if it please you, by a footpath on the right, high above the carriage-way. It is a lovers' walk; a deep-green wooded way made for Phillida and Corydon. Boughs interlace above; the hare-bell, the fox-glove, and the blade-like fern are at our feet; at our side behold the beautiful chalice of the giant campanula, the cup of the golden cistus, the blue eyes of the forget-me-not; the wind brings us messages of scent from azalea, and woodbine, and wild sweet-cicely. Now the path descends under an aisle of rhododendron and pine, and ever and anon a mighty tree has thrown its network of fibrous roots across the wooded walk, till we are brought out at Goyts Bridge, again; Goyts Bridge which might have been the inspiration of Longfellow when he drew that pen-picture where :

> *Reflected in the tide the grey rocks stand,*
> *And trembling shadows throw;*
> *And the fair trees lean over side **by side**,*
> *And see themselves below.*

Our stroll, my friend, **has** occupied **more time** than I thought, for when we scramble down the steep wooded bank of the river, with the lace-like leaf-shadows falling athwart the winsome water, Somebody has got the outline of a pretty vignette on her canvas, and there are already three brace of fine trout in the Young Man's creel. It does one good to see the Young Man whip the water; to witness the light easy graceful touch with which he drops the cast on the stream with the gentleness of gossamer; the adroitness with which the flies are thrown upon hanging leaves on the bank and made to naturally alight on the river; the ease with which he floats the yellow dun May flies over the rising fish, the quick, dexterous, almost imperceptible, turn of the wrist as he sees the suck of the pearl-tipped mouth and strikes; and the subtle skill with which he plays a valorous fellow of at least a pound—the diplomatic lowering of the point of the rod when the fish, feeling the prick of the tempered barb, attempts an aerial evolution, and the ready running out of the line when he makes a frantic rush—a downward flight to release himself—until the speckled beauty has the landing net put under him, and presently lies among the cool grasses on the bank, with that sweet evanescent musk-like aroma about his plump body, which seems to dry off with the water. And I contrast this "judicious Hooker" with the Cockney unaccountables, who, with wonderful armaments in the way of rods and tackles, affect the "Peacock at Wousley," as they call Rowsley. I mind me of one of those superlative superfine gentry once getting up the Wye as far as Bakewell Bridge—I remember he was encased in awkward fishing boots, exasperatingly new; he had a white hat with a marvellous piscatorio-entomological museum of flies wound around it, a stupid muslin veil,— puggarees, don't they call those effeminate abominations?—kept the sweet, glad, sunshine from his poor, dear, tallow-coloured neck; a landing-net and gaff were fixed vertically behind his back; a bran new creel encumbered his shoulders; he wore an impossible belt and an unaccountable pouch, while on his long, lithe rod was affixed a patent winch that made a clicking sound like the wheel of a steam crane. A wonderful man; the promise was tremendous; the performance terrible. His flies fell in the water with a splash like a big brickend; then the line was jerked back for the gut to become entangled, a Gordian knot of difficulty, in an unoffending elder bush that grew over the wall behind. The caustic village humourists, hanging over the bridge, laughed at the perspiring piscator, who lost his temper and his tackle, and instead of fish caught nothing but foliage. Very different is the Young Man, cool of body, calm of mind, and cunning of hand, with his two silken flies, so temptingly natural that they impose upon us, much more the trout, and his half dozen yards of line, working up the narrow stream between the hanging bushes, and leaving hardly an inch of water unfished. A trout is, indeed, a fish worthy of an able rodster. A fish with the pride and instincts, the taste and tone of a gentleman. A fish dignified and dainty, aristocratic and handsome, who grovels not in muddy ponds and in sluggish, slimy streams, leaving the stench of the canal, and the taint of the river to plebeian and coarser natures, electing waters that are clear and crystal, and bounding with cascades, and sheltered with rocks and trees. A fish dauntless, daring, and full of resource, who demands the highest skill and nerve from his antagonist, and is oftener victor than vanquished, snaring the angler instead of the angler snaring him. An epicurean fish, who prefers the graceful fly or the silvery minnow, before nasty greaves and grubs, lob-worms and maggots. An artistic fish, who revels in wild mountain scenery, and fixes his home in the still green solitudes of deep sylvan valleys, where the only sound is the shout of the waterfall and the sweet cadence of the current.

But lo! We have been following the Young Man down the river, and Somebody is left sketching behind in solitude. She is surely as dainty a picture as the scene she is transferring to canvas, this fair Derbyshire girl with the frank clear eyes, and the friendly laughing mouth, in the bright, happy, early, summertime of life, just like the opening ferns and blossoming flowers and newly-budded boughs that frame her portrait, as she sits at her easel in the lonely loveliness, with the glad June light about her, and the swift voiceful river flowing at her feet as it hurries down from the hills from rock to rock, now altogether hid by jealous foliage, and now shining in patches of blue in an opening among the trees.

We apologise for our desertion.

"Oh, I have had lots of company," she laughs. "I have had the society of a linnet and two tomtits picking up crumbs from my dress; and then a great stupid pre-Raphaelite bull, with perverted artistic tastes, came and began inspecting the sketch, finally pointing his opinions with his nose, and **smelling at** the wet colours like an ignorant art-critic, and I had to drive him away with **my mahl** stick, although if he had only kept still I should like to have included him in the picture; while the river has been chatting to me all the time."

It is a pretty picture **whose beauty our lady artist** is throwing upon **the canvas. A reach of river** showing bright and glassy **over a** dark rocky bed; **a** grey stone bridge **where a** tributary **rivulet adds its** clear water; at the **side of** the old arch a gritstone cottage, with **filmy** peat **smoke mixed up among** ragged pine **trees**; a glimpse, and only a glimpse of **brown moor** beyond. It is **a** suggestive bit of "silent poetry," **full of** light and **air** and whisperings of the sweet coolness of green trees and running **water**; a picture to be hung up **in a** curtained room in a far-off town sometime, may be, to take the mind back to this pleasant, peaceful Derbyshire solitude, when in a place, and amid associations, **far** removed from those which inspired the painter.

All too soon does the early summer day pass away; and when **the Young Man** with fairly filled creel summons us to pack up, there is still much to be done to the picture, and so it and easel and palette and tubes of colour and sheaf of brushes are left at the gritstone cottage. To-morrow we hope to treat ourselves to another excursion to Errwood. And to-night as we ride back, the clearness of the skies, and the sharp distinct outlines of the hills, hold out pleasant promises for the day.

A DERBYSHIRE VALLEY IN THE SPRING TIME.

When will the songs be old that tell of spring?
Of buttercups that blow and birds that sing?
Ah, never may my losses or my gains
Make common things to me of fields and lanes!
Guy Roslyn.

The present writer was once called upon for his sins to answer for a charming young lady a series of impertinent questions in what she was pleased to call her "Confession Book." It was demanded from the P.W., for instance, that—following the laudable example of the aforesaid C.Y.L.'s "sisters, her cousins, and her aunts"—he should record his opinion in black and white of what constituted an ideal man and an ideal woman; that he should state what his age was, and whether he was ever in love, and if so, how often; that he should give to the world his direct fiat as to what time of life people should marry, and whether they should unite for love or lucre; that he should confess what was his favourite poem and his favourite hero and heroine in fiction, together with the opera of his choice and the particular colour of his fancy. And among other such inquisitorial queries, wrung from the victim by his fair tormentor was this: "What is the most beautiful thing in nature?" Of course the P.W. wrote that his bright-eyed interlocutor was; but after that dulcet divinity he was fain to confess came A Derbyshire Valley in the Spring Time.

Months have passed since then, Winnie, but I endorse that opinion this May afternoon, as the birds sing to me, and the river wimples on its glassy way, in one of the most beautiful and least known of Derbyshire dales. A couple of hours ago I was a toiler within office walls, with maps and diagrams that insisted with grating emphasis that two and two are four, and could not be five or three under any possible circumstances; the windows looked out upon roaring foundries and big workshops of scrofulous brick; the furniture consisted of precise rows of official shelves filled with my genuine "works," as Charles Lamb, with gay gravity, was wont to say of the bulky daybooks and ledgers of the East India

House. But now there is a soft sky of blue above, faintly flecked with pearl, pleasing colours around, and grassy carpet beneath; the wind brings a welcome of scent from red hawthorn and rain-washed wild flowers; white rocks gleam from a setting of emerald green, and a voiceful river, which intersects the valley like a line of light, is singing a "song without words." Forest, hill, and streamlet mingle in picturesque variety. This morning the forest was one of smoking chimneys; the hills were of coal, and coke, and stacked timber; the stream was a stagnant fermentation of filth denominated a canal; there was the din of industry, the clanging of hammers, the shriek of steam whistles, the sob and wail of tortured metal; revolving wheels suggested "perpetual motion;" everywhere was the sense of brick-and-mortar bondage. This afternoon a delicious Derbyshire dale; an exquisitely tinted picture of rock and river, tor and torrent; a light, thin, buoyant atmosphere; a green gladness soothing the work-wearied eye; and the music of birds and bees, rustling wood, rippling water, and splashing fish, falling gently on town-tried ear. What a welcome transition it is, and how great the contrast between God's Country and man's town! What a quiet haven in a troubled sea; what a sweet truce in the severe fight; what a shady refuge in the feverish race!

It is the fashion for superfine writers to protest with forcible feebleness against railways; but for the line, however, he who was the Theseus of toil two hours ago, doomed to keep for ever in a sitting posture, could not have been the lazy lotus-eater of the limestone dale. The train deposited me at a well known station on the Midland system between Derby and Manchester. I am not, however, going to divulge the name of the station, for such thoughtlessness would betray the whereabouts of my beautiful unknown valley. The Mexicans, who are aware of a city of gold, keep the secret closely to themselves, lest the prying and profane should step in and despoil it of its untold treasures. My hidden valley is only three pleasant miles from where crowded excursion trains of sensational length deposit invading armies of cheap trippers, together with those modern Goths and Vandals who call themselves "Field Naturalists." The unlovely *debris* of paper-bags and ginger-beer bottles, which marks the festive footsteps of the former, is even more tolerable than the wholesale sacking of ferns and flowers which characterises the forages of the latter. " Dovedale is already stripped " to the bare rock of its ferns!" is the lament of the Rev. Gerald Smith, the author of *The Ferns of Derbyshire*, indignant at the rapacious robbers who " rudely tear the ferns from their home so as to

"swell the spoils of a day's excursion, but who as
"rudely cast them off when the day's pleasure is
"past, or plant them in soil and situations where
"they must inevitably pine and die." Legislation
has given us a Wild Birds' Preservation Act. Could
not the life of many a coy fern and modest flower be
saved by a Wild Flowers' Preservation Act? But
this *en passant*. Happily my hidden valley is free
from the presence of both the cheap-tripper and
"field naturalist." It knows not the defilement of
the one or the other. Your Excellency may walk
the whole length of the valley, from where the little
limpid laughing river rises, to where it enlarges the
Wye, without meeting a person, unless it be a keeper
in velveteens, with a gun and dog, who has a civil
good day for respectable folk. It would, indeed,
seem an act of sacrilege for 'Arry to pollute the
lovely loneliness. 'Arry, with his sweetheart, who
wears a discordant bonnet of violent colours, is at
the station as we leave it. They are off to one of
the ducal show places on the beaten track, and are
already receiving the attentions of the raucous-voiced
'bus drivers, who wait for the unwary outside the
station gates.

We turn to the left and over the ancient river
bridge: a grey, quaint, old-world bit of architecture,
whose lichened-stained, moss-grown arches repeat

F

themselves, crumbling stone for crumbling stone, in the Wye, a swift glassy stream beneath, in which you can count the pebbles and the trout, so clear is the unpolluted water. Over the bridge, an hostelry that is another old-world bit of architecture, also grey, quaint, moss-grown, and lichen-stained. It is a picture rather than a place; a ballad sooner than a building; a song in stone; a poem in its deep pointed gables, its antique mullioned windows, its little diamond panes, its clustering chimneys, and its projecting porch. The ivy clings lovingly to this old ideal hostel; and the charm of bygone association lingers, like a perfume, in every room.

> "'Tis a finely-toned picturesque, sunshiny place,
>   Recalling a dozen old stories:
> With a rare British, good-natured, ruddy-stoned face,
>   Suggesting old wines and old Tories:
> Ah, many a magnum of rare crusted port,
>   Of vintage no one could cry fie on,
> Has been drunk by good men of the old-fashioned sort
>   At the ———"

Stay! I was nearly letting out the secret of our location, and that would never do. What a vignette the building makes in the spring sunshine, with the flowing river by its side, and the wooded hills in the background that stand out in the clear bright air with distinct outline and delicate colour. The old inn seems to be a relic of the past bequeathed to the present. You half expect to see people dressed in old-fashioned costumes—in brave cavalier hats with plumes, in stately cloaks, and wearing swords and ruffles—lounging round the carved stone porch, tossing off beakers of wine. The russet building carries your mind back for generations; but you are speedily brought back to unpleasant remembrance of the 19th century, eighth decade, by the appearance at the door of a demonstrative fly fisherman, with loudly displayed calves, who is palpably dressed for the effective pose of his part. Leave we this sartorial exquisite, for whom honest-hearted, simple-minded Izaak Walton would have had a strong repugnance, and pass the little grey thatched houses mixed up among the trees. Genuine rustic cottages, these, and not the "Brummagem" pinch-beck pretenders that Mr. Buggins, the builder, tries to pass current for "cottages" in suburbs of bricklaying barbarisms. A mile and a half of turnpike, through a pastoral country, on which the eye rests on soft woods covering gentle slopes. A river bridge marks a boundary, where the little crystal river we are going to seek falls into the Wye. As we leave the turnpike and turn down a lane to the left, on which the grass and wild flowers encroach on either side, as if jealous of the cartway, we have a vision of grey old towers rising out of a deep mass of wooded hill. Baronial towers, those, eloquent of merry mediæval times. Those time-stained turrets look down on great dining-hall that erst echoed to the loyal shout of feudal retainers; on ball-room with deep oriel windows, where a dozen partners could linger after the dance without one pair seeing the other; on stately terrace where gay hawking parties have gathered; and on—most poetical relic—classic doorway and steps down which tradition says tripped a runaway girl to meet a brave lad, whose elopement is every bit as romantic as that of Lochinvar, Lord Ullin's daughter, or Jock o' Hazeldean.

Our companion for the next mile along the left-hand side of the lane is the little river that gives its name to the valley where we are to sit and dream the afternoon away. It is a typical trout stream, made up of clear rough hurried water, and it contains more trout than all the other Derbyshire streams put together, thanks to the rigid preservation of the Duke of Rutland. It crosses the road at a stone bridge with curious little arches, where another trout haunted mountain brook joins company. And here is an old village, secluded and somnolent, that might belong to Shakespeare's time. Honeysuckles at porches; old-fashioned gardens, with stocks, London pride, pansies, mignonette, nasturtiums, and gillyflowers; thatched roofs, with the sun searching out the mosses and lichens; sweet repose and quiet shadowy nooks and corners everywhere. Here is the farm-house in whose yard on a memorable morning in personal history, I left a canvas bag, containing trout tackle and a pigeon pie for the dinner of two of us, while we went indoors and rested and refreshed ourselves in the best room with mighty draughts of new milk, and said pretty things to the farmer's daughter, who wore a muslin dress and had quite a bouquet of wild roses in her cheeks. When we were so occupied, two hungry harriers were interesting themselves in the canvas bag, and when we came into the yard, ready to proceed on our journey, one of the dogs was making satisfactory progress in the demolition of the pie, while the other animal was dancing in energetic pain with a fish-hook in his tongue! Past this farm-house and through the fields, lilac with the "lady-smocks" at our right. Another time-toned bridge through which the river rushes as through a sluice; a stretch of level meadows that give way presently to the deep shade of wooded paths; the banks gather closer and hug the river, and anon rise high and steep and shut it in on either side, and lo! we are in possession of the Secret Valley.

And the beauty and wonder of the Spring Time are all around. Autumnal tints have their glory;

but look at the variety of this young foliage; the changes that are rung upon green, the tender hesitating yellows, and the light and shade of the pines and firs. Up the mass of that steep wooded slope a wave of green seems to have spread, leaving black unrelieved patches here and there that bring out the new colour with pronounced vividness. The balsam poplars are a golden yellow; there is the rich hue of the copper beech; the oak buds are red. The delicate silver spray-like leaves of the lady birch twinkle in the sunshine like dancing motes of light; and the new palm-like foliage of the larch, drooping from a trunk as slim and straight as the mast of a schooner, is an idyll of colour in its tender, translucent, luminous green. Yes, there is quite as much variety in the foliage of Spring as in the tints of Autumn; and while the latter is a saddening sermon telling of decay and decline, falling leaves, fading flowers, and fleeting light, Spring is eloquent of youth and love, hope and promise, careless confidence and audacious courage. The ferns are opening their fronds in obedient response to the call of the birds, although many of them are still curled up like fiddle-heads among the withered bracken. The sunlight falls in leaf-shadows on tangled paths of wild flowers. There are hyacinths, trembling anemones, and a wealth of blue bells; there are the coral beads of the bilberry, and the pearl shell-like flower of the wood-sorrel, with its little shamrock-shaped leaves that make such a sour impromptu salad. There are lilies of the valley, too, together with white starwort and crimson campion; but your Excellency, whom I know to be a Liberal, will be pleased to note that the prevailing complexion of the flowers is Yellow. It is as if Nature were rejoicing with the Reform Club at the Radical victory at the General Election and were wearing, in consequence, the winning colours. In these glades behold the gold of the daffodil, the amber of the cowslip, the pale yellow of the primrose, the chrome of the marsh marigold, the bright yellow of the little celandine, the vivid yellow of the buttercup. And are not the poplars yellow, and other trees a yellowish green? Yellow, moreover, is the tulip, and lemon tinted are the sunset skies of Spring. The old lines must be reversed:—

> "*For blue is forsaken,*
> *And green is forsworn,*
> *And yellow is the sweetest*
> *Colour that's worn.*"

The sun which is opening leaf and blossom has the same influence upon the birds. What a concert it is, mingled with the murmuring music of the river, and the lullaby that lurks in the trees. The blackbird is whistling on the other side the stream, and the thrush is answering him on this side; a peggy-white-throat, no bigger than a leaf, is trying a duet with a tom-tit in the next tree. That profound egotist and self-advertiser, the cuckoo, is telling the woods its name; and the lark—most spiritual of birds—a speck of song in the blue above, has taken the news of opening summer to the skies. There is the crow of the pheasant in the deep wooded way, and the scream of the jay as it flies past a patch of bright blue. Here is a little bird worth studying. It is the tree tit-lark. It flies up to a topmost branch from the ground, and then comes down in a sweet vibration of song, which just starts and finishes with the fluttering descent. Another moment, and the modest little songster flies up once more, again to come down in a ripple of music. As we walk up the stream the shining white cliffs on either side rise steeper and more sheer, and the growth of wood is denser. Here and there the river has been dammed up into little lochs, and the trout in these deep pools surprise one by their number and their size. Majestic fellows some of them, three and four pounders, lying with their pretty heads poised up stream to catch what the current brings down; or jumping up with a great splash at a succulent fly; or lurking under tree roots to dart out into mid-water whenever there is a temptation. Next to the number of the trout, the clearness of the water surprises the explorer in the Secret Valley. It is perfectly crystal, and as clear now as when Charles Cotton described it to "Viator" in *The Compleat Angler* as "by many "degrees the purest and most transparent stream "that I ever yet saw, either at home or abroad, and " breeding the reddest and best trouts in England." This delicate clearness is caused by the limestone bed through which the river flows, and also through the absence of man on the banks to pollute it with his money-making manufactures. The only habitation in the valley is the keeper's house halfway up. Beyond are the ruins of some old lead workings, with the remains of a tumbled-down aqueduct that once strode across the brightly running water. A mile further up the voiceful valley. In the wildest part, where the solitude is most impressive, and the silence most musical with birds, the river starts a mere spring from a mossy rock, and sets off with great haste to grow from rill to rivulet and rivulet to river. Close by here is a square, stout-built, old farmhouse of warmly-tinted stone, which has been in possession of the same Quaker family these two or three hundred years. There is an honest welcome for us, and bread and cheese and beer—home-baked, home-made, home-brewed, hearty and wholesome— or milk, if your Excellency prefer it. Our respects to you, Farmer Bowman.

And now comes a stride across the fields with the plover distracting our attention from its nest among the long grasses by shrill cries of "pee-wit," which are almost painful in their earnest anxiety; anon a village, not particularly picturesque, straggling and generally exposed, hungry-looking and stony; and then two or three miles tramping along a lonely turnpike, blinding white and very dusty, with limestone walls dissecting fields that seem to grow limestone boulders as big as sheep; then a grand old church, where those runaway lovers, I spoke of when we started, sleep in a last long embrace that knows no parting; and then, behold! a quaint mediæval market town, with the repose and poetic shadows of the centuries hanging about its dreamy public square and its narrow streets filled up with glints of green. Pleasant it is to step into the openings of the river bridge and watch the fishermen below, and trace the windings of the Wye, which wanders in splashes of light in the green breadths of meadow, giving to the landscape by its wilful sinuosities alternate glances of flood and field. Turn where we will there is something pleasant for the eye to rest upon, be it the clear flowing river, with the broad path by its bank, where the growing youth and garrulous age of the place loiter in the soft sunset light; or the swelling ducal woods beyond, which tuck in the town on every side; or the old-fashioned houses of grey stone or mellow brick with red tiles, that speak of rest and peace. All too soon does the train time come. All too soon is the brief truce in the battle over. All too soon we shall reach the actual jostling, greedy, sterile, unsympathetic world.

> "*O no, I do not wish to see*
>   *The sunshine o'er these hills again;*
> *Their quiet beauty wakes in me*
>   *A thousand wishes wild and vain.*
>
> . . . . . .
>
> *And fancies from afar are brought*
>   *By magic lights and wandering wind;*
> *Such scene hath poet never sought*
>   *But he hath left his heart behind.*
>
> *It is too sad to feel how blest*
>   *In such a spot might be our home;*
> *And then to think with what unrest*
>   *Throughout this weary world we roam.*"

AT CHANTREY'S GRAVE.

"*Hillsborough, though built on one of the loveliest sites in England, is perhaps the most hideous town in creation . . . The city is pock-marked with public-houses, and bristles with high, round chimneys . . . They defy the law, and belch forth massy volumes of black smoke, that hang like acres of crape over the place, and veil the sun and the blue sky even in the brightest day; but in a fog—why, the air of Hillsborough looks a thing to plough, if you want a dirty job. More than one crystal stream runs sparkling down the valleys, and enters the town; but they soon get defiled, and creep through it heavily charged with dyes, clogged with putridity, and bubbling with poisonous gases, till at last they turn to mere ink, stink, and malaria, and people the churchyards as they crawl. This infernal city, whose water is blacking, and whose air is coal, lies in a basin of delight and beauty: noble slopes, broad valleys, watered by rivers and brooks of singular beauty, and fringed by fair woods in places.*"

CHARLES READE.

"The foulest town in the fairest country I have ever seen." Such was Horace Walpole's terse description of Sheffield. It hits off the cutlery capital more happily, perhaps, at the present time than when it was first written. Sheffield itself only grows bigger and blacker, duller and dirtier, and its sordid streets only bring out in stronger relief its romantic suburbs. A blurred, blotted, seamed, smoked, disfigured picture in an attractive frame; the ill-conditioned daub only draws attention to its beautiful enclosure. Sheffield supplies a humiliating illustration of man's town and God's Country. No town had a finer site given to it for effective architecture. One sighs to think to what picturesque purpose a Norman Shaw might have turned such natural advantages. Sheffield itself is a hill surrounded by investing lines of nobler hills, with three rivers, forming three sides of a peninsulated area, upon which spreads the town, and there is not a street in the place from which a glimpse of the country may not be seen. The town is as hideous as positive genius for the perverse perpetration of deformed ugliness can make it; but the hilly suburbs, with their wooded valleys, possess a scenic charm which it is difficult to imagine existing in such close contact with so much that is revolting and contaminating. These are the valleys of the Sheaf and the Don, the glens of quiet beauty such as the Eden, the Loxley, and the Rivelin.

> "*Five rivers like the fingers on a hand,*
> *Flung from black mountains, mingle and* ***are one***
> *Where sweetest valleys quit the wild and grand.*"

The Rivelin ravine, with its bold hills stretching westward to the Derbyshire moors, is a romance; and here Mr. Ruskin has placed his St. George's Museum, just where the comparison between God and man is seen in the most vivid contrast. Then there is the valley of **the** Don, with the warbling woodlands of Wharncliffe, the view from which Lady **Mary** Montague, writing from Avignon, placed before the landscape at the junction **of** the Rhone and Durance, the beauty of which she was describing. "Last summer," she says, "in the hot evenings, I "walked often thither, where I always found a fresh "breeze, and the most beautiful land prospects I ever "saw, *except Wharncliffe*, being a view of the wind- "ings of two great rivers, and overlooking the whole "country, with part of Languedoc and Provence." But the most attractive part of Hallamshire lies in Derbyshire. Sheffield, indeed, had a narrow escape to get into Yorkshire at all. Part of the town is in Derbyshire; and the valley of the Sheaf belongs to the Peake countrie entirely. Beauchieff Abbey *(beau chef:* "beautiful head") lies in this fair vale, with shady woods encompassing it, and the great space and solitude **of the** Derbyshire moors beyond. **And** overlooking the Sheaf valley, perched like an eyrie on the hill, is Norton; classic Norton: the rugged **Derbyshire** village where Sir Francis Chantrey **was** born, where he toiled an obscure milk-boy, where he cherished his earliest artistic dreams, where his widowed mother always lived, and where her fond and famous son lies buried.

I have often been struck with the antipodean contrast between the brutal uncouthness of Sheffield, and the romantic comeliness of its natural surroundings. The antithesis, however, has never impressed me so forcibly as it does as I leave Sheffield with Orestes, an old comrade-in-arms, this sunny morning at the end of May, to stroll as far as the Church associated with Chantrey's immortality. It is a pleasant walk of four or five miles from Sheffield High Street to Norton. When we have left Heeley we are away from the low tenements, suffering from a brick-and-mortar erysipelas, the arid workshops, seamed with a scrofula of dirt, the foul chimneys that vomit at the sun, the vitiated rivers that once were trout haunted streams, and were kissed by hanging greenery, and leapt with joy **in the** sunshine, but now crawl wearily, heavy with pestilence. Now the glad green country is all around us. A great breadth of transparent blue is in the sky; the pure thin air is full of exhilarating light; the outward aspect of **Nature** is one that would have inspired pæans of praise from Sheffield's native singers, Montgomery and Elliott. Yet it is but a step from this earthly Heaven to that mercantile, metallic Hades: to the Styx, the Cocytus, and the Acheron; to the heavy atmosphere of Pluto's Kingdom, where the one-eyed Cyclops, with the flaming foreheads, are beating molten metal till it wails and moans in the very agony of torture.

We turn through the fields to the left as we approach Ecclesall. That grey village on the wooded hill overlooking the valley is Norton. Norton itself is a scattered place. Here is a collection of old rustic houses, with one or two modern villas, painfully new and largely little, that reach the height of their paltry architectural ambition when they throw out a self-assertive bow window, almost as big as the house itself; together with a little post office, and a public-house that is styled "The Chantrey Arms," and combines the sale of both bread and beer, grog and groceries. At this establishment we learn that the actual Norton is "ar gud moil from 'ere," and that we shall have to "go thru' th' jennel and then thru' th' wood." "Th' jennel" turns out to be a passage between two houses. This funnel gives access to open fields. Now comes a stiff climb up to a glorious old wood, bright with blue-bells. The view from here is a revelation in landscape. Far away below lies the foul blot of Sheffield in a fair country where hills rise on hills and valleys meet in valleys. A pall of smoke broods mournfully over the town. Right across are the moors of the Peak, breaking in waves of heather to the horizon; to Hathersage and Grindleford Bridge, to Froggatt Edge and Baslow. Orestes denotes for my delectation the different localities in the borough of Sheffield that now is stretched like a map below. That smoky smudge, a dusky yellow in the sunshine, is Attercliffe; that black place is with cruel irony named Brightside; yonder is pleasant Nether Edge; there Sharrow; there Crooks; there hilly Steel Bank and Walkley. And then he points out this and that beautiful mansion mixed up among trees. That he notes with great precision is the seat of Mr. Polyphemus Bessemer Pigg, of the firm of Messieurs Arges, Brontes, and Steropes, Unlimited; yonder is the suburban seat of Mr. Vulcan Cœlus, J.P., senior partner of the wonderful Sulphurous Brimstone and Steam Hammer Company; there resides Mr. Alderman Ferruginous Terra, who boasts that he "made his brass by dirt." These are the Iron Princes who take the life of the crystal streams, who gash with ugly scars fair scenes, and whose workmen are herded together in sordid dwellings, with open drains in front, that it would be monstrous to describe by the sweet name "home." Notice, my friend, that the men who prosper out of deformity **live far out of** the demoralisation of Nature themselves. They seek delightful little "beauty-spots" of their own. They are "the heads of the people," those they employ are often only—" hands."

Through the wood, and on to a pleasant country road, where more of the village of Norton is scattered. Entirely old this part. Mr. Buggins, the builder, has not yet put down any of his bricklaying barbarisms, his architectural atrocities. Here is a grey old farm-house where little boy Chantrey probably played with other milk-boys; and I believe there still exists, though in an altered form, outside the village, the low-roofed humble house where the great sculptor was born. Presently comes Norton Hall— there are splendid prospects in the Park—then, on the roadside to the left, an old-fashioned English mansion which you associate with a fine old Tory; then more antique houses, mixed up in the deep shade of woods, a poet's fancy of grey roof, green tree, and filmy smoke. Then the venerable church itself. On the village green, which at first seems part and parcel of the churchyard, so closely does the plot of grass adjoin the sacred enclosure, is a commanding obelisk. It is a single shaft of unpolished Cheesewring granite. There is no carved design. The only inscription is the boldly cut word,

CHANTREY.

Yet plain as the obelisk is, it occurs to us that the very plainness is Art itself, and far better in its severe simplicity than any sculptured piece that would have only challenged comparison with the masterwork of the English Phidias whose genius it aspired to commemorate. We have only to step across the little patch of sward to gain access to the churchyard. Moss-grown and still is this secluded God's acre, shut in with the trees of Norton Park. The old church looks like a tradition in stone, so old and shadowy does it appear in the green shade. There is the light translucent tender tint of May on the trees, mingled with the hesitating yellow of the opening oak leaves, and the dark red of the copper beech, and shaded with the gloomy hue of yews, which have kept sombre vigil over the dead for centuries. A country churchyard is always an interesting study, even to minds less tinged with melancholy than a Blair's or a Hervey's. The silence has an eloquence of its own. As Doctor Raleigh in a fine passage puts it, "Nature seems to concentrate her pathos and her stillness in such a spot. Quiet is the dust below; quiet the scarcely moving grass of the graves; quiet the shadows of the tombstones; quiet the over-arching sky; and he who sits there on the mouldering stone, looking at the graves of his kindred, is thinking: 'It is a quiet resting-place; I shall not be sorry when the toils of this life are over, and wearied I come in hither to lay me down among the rest. I shall be glad rather when the sowing and the reaping are done, and I am brought here like as a shock of corn cometh in his season.'"

Norton churchyard is especially attractive to one who derives a quiet pleasure in studying quaint verses, and deciphering old country-side names. Here is a portion of an old cross, starting a shattered shaft from four circular steps; here is a newly-made grave, with the fresh soil yet wet with weepers' tears; and here, tree-shaded and unobtrusive, is the grave of Chantrey. Two flat granite slabs in a railed enclosure, plain but polished, and with the lettering boldly and deeply cut. The slabs are of unequal size. The larger covers all that is mortal of the great sculptor. Thus reads the inscription:—

Sir Francis Chantrey,
Sculptor,
R.A.   F.R.S.

Born in this Parish VII. April, MVCCLXXXI.

Died in London, Nov. XXV., MVCCCXXXI.

The smaller slab covers the ashes of his grandfather, his father, and his mother, and the lettering reads:

M.
Francis Chantrey
Died MVCCLXVI, aged LVI.

FRANCIS CHANTREY
Died MVCCXCIII, aged XXXXV.
SARAH, His Wife,
Died MVCCCXXVI, age LXXXI.

Sir Francis might have reposed among the honoured dead in the historic Abbey; or beside Reynolds and **Barry in the** Cathedral; but he elected that his ashes should rest with his country-side kith and kin in the simple old-world village, where he, a poor fatherless boy, worked on a humble farm and trudged with his milk-cans to Sheffield. The story of his life is a romance. The Norton milk-boy's first inspirations were sketched on a grinder's wall. Then the milk-boy became a carver and gilder's apprentice in Sheffield—the dolorous town which I have said is the grave rather than the cradle of artistic hopes, and where fact—hard, grinding, **and** repellent—crushes out fancy, beautiful, ennobling, and graceful. In the leisure hours of his apprenticeship **the** boy Chantrey drew and **modelled in a room** which he hired weekly for a few pence. Then he left to struggle with difficulties in Dublin, and push on endeavours at Edinburgh. Then London, where he met Nollekins, who smoothed for him the steep and stony chequered path. Then he " struck for honest fame," and after vain effort came victory, after trial triumph. Then surfeited with fame, came the desire to slumber, not amid the mighty great ones in the national Walhalla, but to rest amid the repose and silence and soothing shadows of this sequestered village churchyard of his boyhood.

We find the church old and interesting. Part of it dates from the late Norman period, being built by one Robert Fitz Ranulph, in the time of Henry II.; the rest of the building belongs to the Perpendicular Period; but everything about the place is quaint and mediæval, and carries the mind back hundreds of years to when the monks fasted and feasted in the adjacent abbey of Beauchieff. The pews are high and old-fashioned; the sun falls gently on the recumbent alabaster effigies of William Blythe and his wife, dressed in the habit of the fifteenth century; there are more mouldering monuments of this Blythe family, one of whom, Geoffrey, was, in 1503, Bishop of Lichfield; all around the dead speak to you through the eye; while there is a curious font of early English Art, standing upon four groups of pillars, with a strange carving, with a bird's body, a reptile's tail, and a human face, the latter wearing an expression of extreme mortification, which is supposed to symbolise Satan and his dislike to the sacrament of Christian baptism. The weight of centuries seems to rest upon the church; and there is the solemnity of years about the walls, even though the May sunshine streams down the aisles, and the new leaves tap at the windows and tell of Spring, and Hope, and Promise.

We wander amid the shadowy nooks and corners of the somnolent, moss-grown village. Its soothing quiet acts like a charm. Its hush and repose, and the gentle beauty of its deep wooded ways, invite the jaded mind, the vexed heart, and the disappointed life. Before long we must rest in its sweet shelter again, and thank God that there is still left in the very heart of industrial England a spot where man may bury the memory of vain ambitions and bitter failures and futile successes, may forget the illusions of life and the fallacies of hope, and may rebuild with surer foundation those castles in the air which have fallen down with such a pitiless crash and well-nigh buried their builder in the ruin.

OVER THE HIGH PEAK RAILWAY.

*"No poetry in railways! foolish thought
Of a dull brain to no fine music wrought."*

"Once upon a time," in the pages of a popular art magazine, the present writer, with a presumption that must have been regarded as a literary impertinence by the æsthetic exquisites who are full of Mr. Matthew Arnold's vague gospel of "sweetness and light," and share Mr. John Ruskin's honest contempt for "kettles on wheels," endeavoured to depict the romantic side of railways. He tried to show that a railway—unyielding, noisy, repellent, and dirty—had in its hard reality an intimate connection with poetry, music, tenderness, sentiment, and art; that pictures are to be seen in trains; that aching tragedies and diverting comedies are ever to be beheld on busy railway platforms, and at little wayside country stations. He was wishful to find poetry in points and crossings, sermons in steel rails, songs in sleepers, books in block signal-boxes, tongues in tunnels, and romance in all railway things. There can be no doubt that the Present Writer ought to have been punished for so flagrant a piece of printed audacity by being suitably maimed in a railway collision, or sent over the Tay Bridge with that awful "flash of light" on that tragic December night at the close of 1879. "Prisoner at the Bar"—is reported to have said a famous Justice of the Peace, surer of his genius than his grammar—"Providence has blessed you with health, strength, and fair abilities, instead of which you go about the country stealing ducks." The railway Juggernaut has not yet called upon me to pay the sacrifice for my sins, "instead of which" I find myself at Whaley Bridge, on Saturday, July 10th, 1880, still pursuing the romance of railways, and about to take a trip on the engine over the High Peak Line, a privilege for which I am indebted to the Engineer of the London and North-Western Company.

Most tourists in Derbyshire have, I take it, encountered, at some point or another, the acute curves, and sensational gradients of the Cromford and High Peak Railway, and have wondered what the mysterious track was, how it got there,

from whence it started, and to whither it was
directed, and were glad to think that their route did
not include the adventure of those Avernus-like
declines and those sharp bends. For the information
of these good ladies and gentlemen, the present paper
should be prefaced by the remark that the High
Peak Railway is purely used for goods and mineral
traffic, and that passengers are not conveyed by it,
although some years ago the guard was allowed to
take a few people between local stations, but an
accident occurred which closed the privilege. Thirty-
two and a half miles long, this mountain line
connects the Cromford Canal and the Midland
Railway at Whatstandwell, in Derbyshire, with the
Peak Forest Canal and the London and North-
Western system at Whaley Bridge, Cheshire. It
was constructed at a cost of £200,000 as a private
enterprise; but the undertaking did not prove pro-
fitable, and the line was leased eventually to the
London and North-Western Railway Company in
perpetuity. This morning I am to traverse the
whole extent of the line on the engine, or rather
engines, for the railway is divided for working
purposes into eight sections, viz:—High Peak
Junction to Cromford; Summit of Sheep Pasture to
Foot of Middleton; Summit of Middleton to Foot of
Hopton; Summit of Hurdlow to Hurdlow; Hurdlow

to Harpur Hill; Harpur Hill to Grin Branch Junction; Colliery Junction to Bunsall; and Foot of Bunsall to Summit of Shallcross. Some of these names will sound strange to the ear of even the reader who prides himself on his close acquaintance with the Peak district. Off the beaten track, they are like hamlets that have got lost among the hills, and need a special exploring party to discover them. The High Peak Railway, it may be further advanced in the way of preface, is a single line. It is of the same width of gauge, and of the same character of permanent way, as the lines belonging to the London and North-Western Company's ordinary branches. Like all single lines the traffic is worked by what in railway parlance is known as the "staff system." The staff is a truncheon painted and lettered specially for the division of line over which it acts as the *open sesame*. It is suspended on the weather-board of the engine, and no train or engine may enter any section without being in possession of the engine-staff belonging to that section. The driver cannot start without this staff, which he receives from the official in charge of the staff station; and on arriving at the station to which the staff extends, the talisman is given up to the person conducting that place. Through or local, "up" or "down," "fly" or "slow," there are twenty-two trains a day on the High Peak Railway, and the fastest trains occupy a space of over five hours in performing the entire journey. All this I candidly concede, my dear Madam, is very dry and uninteresting, and I apologise for being so tediously technical. The only extenuation I can urge is that the High Peak Railway is in itself a solid fact of such dimensions that a discursive description of it should also be "ballasted" with facts and figures, *data* and detail, to carry even my special light locomotive safely.

I am at Whaley Bridge this July morning; and before half the world has breakfasted, and while housemaids, drowsy and slovenly, are yawningly lighting the fire to prepare the matutinal meal, the through "up" train to Whatstandwell is off and away. Due out at ten minutes past seven o'clock, we are timed to arrive at the Cromford terminus at a quarter past twelve, according to the current time table, which is dated "December, 1876, and until further notice;" an arrangement which is primitive and simple, and makes one wish that the hours of departure and arrival of all trains in "Bradshaw" savoured equally of the unvarying constancy of the Medes and Persians. One leaves Whaley Bridge, with its factories and colliery gins and slag heaps, without regret. The first mile or so of the ride is achieved in the guard's brake, and is up the Shallcross gradient, a straight rise of 1 in 8½. The line is here double, and is worked by an endless chain. Presently we are among the bold features of the Derbyshire moorland hills; and the Goyt on our right is running innocently away between the banks of lichened rock, coy fern, and hanging trees. A locomotive meets us at the summit of the incline, and working tender first is taking on our train of some twenty waggons: a cargo that is a curious *olla podrida* of grains, barrels of beer, bags of beans, sewing machines, flour, lime, coal, cans of paint, boxes of tea, and agricultural implements. To one accustomed to the swift, smooth, motionless motion of a Pullman Palace Car, or a Midland bogie carriage, the jerking, jolting, jig-dancing of the engine of the High Peak Railway is an experience to remember as a certain specific for the cure of indigestion. The seven o'clock breakfast is already shaken down; and no wonder that Toodles, the stoker, is feeding himself as well as the engine. Toodles is a grotesque combination of grit and grease, and might have been carved out of a column of coal and then roughly oiled and toned down; while his "mate," the driver, an older man, is suggestive of an impossible partnership between a butcher and a chimney sweep, wearing—as he does—the blue blouse of the one, and the mosaic of soot of the other.

We are now in full swing; and everything about the train strikes me as being mechanically malevolent, discordant, and out of temper. The engine has not the mellow "fluff-fluff," and the full-voiced, deep-throated "chay-chay," of its superior locomotive brethren, the race horses of the main line. It spits its way along spitefully, and starts with a jerk, and stops with a jump, and goes with an irregular lurch throughout that is trying to one who has not acquired his "sea-legs." The waggons, through not being so closely united in the tightness of "coupling" as they might be, batter away at each other as if each individual truck had quarrelled with its partner, and was settling its grievances in blows. The curves are so sharp and frequent that ever and anon the train seems intent on the study of Euclid's Elements, and describes every denomination of geometrical outline, the favourite one being an acute crescent, when the van at the rear of the train comes up at right angles with the engine just to allow the driver and guard to shake hands, and show that if the engine is ill-tempered, and the waggons are emphatic in their contempt for each other, they, at least, are friends. Now the whole train seems bent on going a trip over the low stone walls into the neighbouring moors to the right; then it evinces that it has changed its mind and has a disposition for toppling over to the left. Between walls of woodbine and ivy now; then to the right, the deep wooded shade of Errwood Hall, as the line runs along a terrace of rock, high over the wild, green, glen beauty of the Goyt Valley. Presently Bunsall is reached. Here the engine leaves us, and the train is pulled in instalments up the steepest gradient of the line, varying from one in seven to one in eight. It is a double one, the first straight, the second on the curve. The operation is a long and tedious one; but at last the whole train is marshalled on the summit. Another locomotive is waiting to take us on, and I am making friends with the two fresh engine men, greasier and grittier than the last, and am learning to balance myself on another quivering foot-board, as we pant through a wild, bleak, hilly country. We seem to be moving along the top of the world; there are deep hollows in the hills below; and every variety of peak and rounded knoll. The journey is a scamper across savage and solitary moors. The heather grows to the verge of the line. The rarefied air blows about you like a fresh sea breeze. The train is the only moving thing in sight, save a wild grouse, when on the wing, rises with a sharp startled cry. Then, just as Buxton is seen, with its white houses lying in the hollow, and shining like a pearl in a setting of emerald, a sudden scream from the engine takes the startled air, and darkness shrouds the speeding train. "Burbage Tunnel," yells Toodles in my ear, as he opens the firebox, and stands like a Salamander in a white dazzling circle of heat. But the wind has hurried away with his words. A thousand echoes are fighting with each other; the wet walls fly past like a rushing river; there is a furious whirlwind of tumult, and a damp chill that might belong to the Styx. The train, indeed, might be Charon's boat; and the driver, standing so statuesque and silent in the broad, blinding circle of white light, with his eye strained in earnest watchfulness, and his hand fixed with decisive hold on the cold glistening regulator, might be Dante's infernal ferryman. In the distance, however, there is hope. A glimpse of light, looking as big as half-a-crown, widens. It grows larger and larger, until, with a wild shriek of exultation from the snorting engine, we emerge from the confined vault, with its darkness and damp, and strange unearthly noises, into the glad blue light and freedom again, and see the windows of Buxton flashing back the sunlight far away below our breezy table-land. Half-a-mile long, the Burbage tunnel is the only one on the High Peak Railway of any importance, and it is dirty enough and wet enough for them all.

"This is Ladmanlow," ventures the driver, shutting off the steam. The information anticipates my query, for there are no name boards on any of the stations to indicate your whereabouts. The stations, indeed, are but sheds; and they sometimes seem to be the only erections within miles of anywhere. Some little time is now occupied in the operation known as "shunting," the dropping of one waggon off, and the coupling of another on; sending this truck down that siding, and fetching that truck from another. After thus playing at a species of truck-tennis with the entire train for some time, we rattle along again. Past Diamond Hill; past the stony slopes of Solomon's Temple; past Harpur Hill, with the tall, insolent, ugly, ubiquitous chimney which threatens the vision of the Buxton visitor wherever he may be, whether on the top of Corbar, or on the slopes of Axe Edge, at the Cat and Fiddle, or at Fairfield. And now the landmarks are lost, and we are running with a rattle and a roar over the moors. Steep are the gradients, and "a caution" are the curves. The engineman treats his iron-horse as if he were driving a living animal. He knows her faults and her good points. He can tell at what part of the road she wants whip and loose rein, and when he must hold her in with tight hand. And the iron Bucephalus

H

responds as if sensitive to his will, and the slightest movement of the regulator is as a touch of spur, and makes her spring on like a creature of blood and nerves. Now a hare starts by the side of the line; now some grouse **rise** with noisy "cluck cluck"; **again a** flight of crows, making for some feeding place, is the only sign of life in the lofty loneliness. Here there are fields **on** either **side of** the rough track; but what the unsophisticated eye takes for sheep grazing are really so many obtruding blocks **of** grey limestone. Hindlow is the next stopping place. "Low" in the Peak district means "high;" and the quaint **old** Derbyshire people describe a residence in these exposed altitudes as "living out of doors." Hurdlow is the succeeding station ("low" again, you see), **and** this is the highest point of the High Peak Line. To get here there was formerly a third incline, but the gradient has been rendered workable by locomotive. A change of guard, and transfer to a third engine, with driver and fireman who can hold their own in grease and grit with their ebony colleagues. There is no water supply at this *depôt*, and to assuage the Iron Horse's thirst, water is brought in large tanks from Ladmanlow. More truck tennis; and then we bump along again; now upon a terrace of rocky embankment; now in a steep cutting, with the naked limestone rocks clothed in flounces of green which you can gather as you pass, so scanty is the clearing; now a sharp whistle of warning from the engine to announce our approach to some platelayers, who leap aside with pick and shovel just in time as we whisk past in a cloud of steam. Anon we rush under a bridge carrying a road that seems to lead nowhere; then we pause at a little one-horse kind of a station called Parsley Hay, which looks just like a wayside shed on an American prairie line. The guard seems to combine the duties of station-master, shunter, clerk, signal-man, porter, and inspector. Indeed, he seems to be the only element of existence about the place. One misses that pleasant aspect of life, that intensely human interest, which belongs to English country-side stations. There is an omission of healthy, unkempt children to see the train pass through. Nobody gets in or out. Where is the stout old lady who is always so anxious about her luggage: three boxes, a portmanteau, and a basket, all with a bit of red flannel tied to the handles? And where is the crimson apoplectic person, with umbrella and carpet-bag, who rushes up to the train just in time to behold it pass away without him? There are none of those little lyrics, those charming pastorals and delicious idylls, one can always observe on village platforms; where lovers meet lovers, and friends say the sad word farewell; where there are kisses at the carriage doors as honeyed as Eros sucked from the lips of Psyche, and tears as scalding as those which dimmed the eyes of Eurydice when Orpheus was snatched from her side. There is not even the stumpy church tower to be seen mixed up in trees, and rising above grey old gabled farm buildings, at these High Peak out-of-the-world stations.

Between Friden and Minninglow is the great Gotham Curve, which describes a rectangular square; and then—quick, if you please!—and you will see, on the left hand, the Arbor Low rocks: hoary Druidical stones. And then, after this glory of the rocks, Toodles screws on his brake, and we stop at Bloore's Siding. Who is Bloore that he should have a siding? He is evidently a man of bricks. But the subject is not one that is likely to throw the world into convulsions of controversy; and the engine is panting away again. The scenery, truth to tell, has not been specially attractive during the last few miles. There have been none of those poetic vignettes of green valley and grey crag, gleaming water and glowing wood, that make the ride in a Midland carriage from Derby to Marple such a rich railway romance. Rather a monotonous table-land, where niggard fields and stubborn heath are ruled off with bleak stone walls, and the perspective is unbroken save here and there by a clump of storm-rent ragged pines. At Longcliffe, however, the views are more diversified; and we get in a pleasant country of hill and dale, with glimpses of wood and water, rendered all the more pleasing to the artistic eye by the sudden lighting up of the picture by the sun, which has been sulking behind grey clouds all day. As Hopton is approached there is some bold rock scenery; and the limestone cuttings show engineering works of great difficulty. Another engine is harnessed to ours here, and with both brakes screwed down, we slide down the incline to Middleton. To think that I have for a moment allowed myself to charge the High Peak Railway with being unpicturesque! *Peccavi*, as the droll commander said when he announced to the First Lord his capture of Scinde, contrary to instructions. Picturesque enough to make me wish to enchant hither the painters by whom it would be most appreciated is the view now, with the Black Rocks of Stonnis, pointing over the Matlock Valley, and Barrel Edge rising in serried ranks of pine and fir above them, and the filmy smoke of peaceful Wirksworth rising lazily from the green-wooded hollow beyond. That Sleepy Hollow is Adam Bede's country; and in the churchyard yonder Dinah Morris awaits the Resurrection bidding. Do you recognise the scene from "the preaching" chapter of George Eliot's first, freshest, and most famous work? "In two or three hours' "ride the traveller might exchange a bleak, treeless, "region, intersected by lines of cold grey stone, for "one where his road wound under the shelter of "woods, or up swelling hills. . . . . High up "against the horizon were the huge conical masses "of hill, like giant moulds intended to fortify this "region of corn and grass against the keen and "hungry winds of the north; not distant enough to "be clothed in purple mystery, but with sombre "greenish sides visibly speckled with sheep, whose "motion was only revealed by memory, not detected "by sight; wooed from day to day by the changing "hours, but responding with no change in them- "selves—left for ever grim and sullen after the flush "of morning, the winged gleams of the April noon- "day, the parting crimson glory of the ripening "summer sun. And directly below them the eye "rested on a more advanced line of hanging woods "divided by bright patches of pasture or furrowed "crops, and not yet deepening into the uniform "leafy curtains of high summer, but still showing "the warm tints of the young oak and the tender "green of the ash and lime."

But there is something else to think about besides

George Eliot now, oh dreamer. There is the Middleton Incline to go down. The locomotive leaves us; and down below drops the shining track of steel, its diminishing lines a study of perspective. The gradient is 1 in 8½; and the train is let down two waggons at a time by a coiled wire rope from a stationary engine. You must be quite prepared to hazard the risk of the run down. Sometimes a waggon *does* break loose, and it will not stop to be reasoned with, but goes to swift destruction. Ride across the buffer my friend, and be prepared to jump off at once if anything gives way. The hook is coupled to the waggons. Off we glide. The cable swings and clangs ominously as it strikes the steel rollers, which seem to say "Caution!" in a metallic voice that keeps repeating itself all the way down. Steeplehouse is the next station; and here *the* view of the line is beheld as, riding on yet another locomotive, we pass directly under the Black Rocks and see through the green veil of the sunlit wood that vision of Matlock, with the deep crags of the Derwent valley, which is like a piece of sublime theatrical scene painting from a romantic opera. There is another of those creepy, dithery inclines at Sheep Pasture, with a gradient on the curve of 1 in 8 down to Cromford; but one forgets the risk of riding on buffers in the green beauty of the scene, for the rocky cutting through which the line winds is a fern paradise that is a revelation of loveliness.

Another locomotive to take the train to High Peak Junction at Whatstandwell. The unique "Oozly bird" came over to this country, it is well known, in two ships; but to get over the High Peak Line involves at least half-a-dozen locomotives. No, thank you very much, Toodles. I will not ride down to the Junction. My bones have been sufficiently dissected; and "The Greyhound" at Cromford is eloquent of a refreshing bath, and of a well-cooked dish of plump trout that were rising at flies in the cool Derwent an hour or so ago.

IN THE KINDERSCOUT COUNTRY.

"*A north-midland shire, dusk with moorland, ridged with mountain . . . . There are great moors behind and on each hand of me; there are waves of mountains far beyond that deep valley at my feet. The population here must be thin, and I see no passengers on these roads: they stretch out east, west, north, and south—white, broad, lonely; they are all cut in the moor, and the heather **grows** deep and wild to their very verge . . . I have no relative but the universal mother, Nature: I will **seek her breast** and **ask** repose . . . I struck straight into **the** heath, I held on to **a** hollow I saw deeply furrowing the brown moorside; I **waded knee-**deep in its dark growth; I turned with **its** turnings, and finding a moss-blackened granite crag **in a** hidden angle, I sat down under it. High **banks of** moor were about me; the crag protected my head; **the** sky was over that.*"

CHARLOTTE BRONTË.

August the Twelfth! Summer—two months behind its time—come at last, and making up for its lateness **by the** warmth of its reception. A day white with heat; the sky steely in its blue brilliance; the air a burning radiance. Everybody off and away to the land of the grouse, or to the cool fresh salt scent of the sea. Everybody departing, except those who have already gone; or those who —like myself—have already eaten their holiday cake; or those—God prosper them!—who never have any holiday cake to eat, and to whom there never comes a truce in the conflict of life, or an armistice in the Battle of Bread. A real hot day. "*H*aint it 'ot? *H*awful 'ot!" as Mr. Middlewick remarks in the play, his *H's* running into each other with heat. I mop my head with my handkerchief; I pick out the shady side of the glaring street; I don't think it effeminate to put up an umbrella to filter the fiery fierceness. The dapper clerks at the Bank are cashing cheques in their shirt-sleeves; the pavements are hot enough to serve the purposes of the humane men who teach young bears to dance; the air pulsates with heat; the dogs are rushing about with hanging tongues horribly suggestive of hydrophobia; claret cup is popular. The only man to be envied is the custodian of the municipal watering cart; and I am almost inclined to carry out one of Mr. Ashby-Sterry's whimsical "warm weather wishes," and bribe that functionary to let me get inside the cart, and allow my head only to be seen through the trap door, whilst in cucumbrian coolness I could jeer at the panting and parched passers by from my delicious retreat.

"*Oh! for a day on a moor!*" I sigh, as the window blinds are pulled down, and I shut myself up in an atmosphere of ink. The postman must have heard the aspiration; for, just as it is expressed, there comes a letter with a familiar post-mark, and addressed by a "fine Roman hand" I have often grasped in greeting and good-bye. It is an invitation to refuse which would subject me to the direst penalties and pains. It comes from the Young Man, before mentioned in these pages, who unites the wisdom and experience of a long and eventful life with the robust strength, the vivacious feeling, and the youthful temperament that belong to the teens. He has refused an invitation to Lord Loamshire's grouse-shooting party, because he thinks the sport cruel, and he has sympathies with the sufferings of the birds which are shot but yet escape to die a lingering painful death in the hidden hollows. But the spirit of grouseland has got possession of him; he must get on the moors; and will I tramp the untrodden Kinderscout country for a couple of days? And is not the invitation endorsed by Somebody, and emphasised by her sister? And is not a sprig of purple heather enclosed in the letter, just to complete the temptation? Man is but mortal, let business plead never so powerfully; and with such weather, and under such circumstances, it is **not long before a** plausible excuse presents itself to justify an escape from **the city.**

The same night the train brings me from the broiling town to **Buxton.** Cool breezes are coming down from the hills to the **crowded Spa,** now in the full **throb of** the season. The next morning is like its predecessor, white with cloudless heat. A fascinating Watteau picture the Gardens and the Pavilion present, with the green trees **mixed** up in the glare **of the sun,** and gay dresses **competing** with bright **flowers in** rivalry of colour. But not **for** us Gounod's melodies; not for us **the** drawling chatter of the rich dawdlers, languidly promenading on the terrace; not for us the trivial lawn tennis; not for us the flirting in Corbar's deep secluded paths of green shade; not for us the grateful waters **of** St. Ann; not for **us the** idle shopping in the Colonnade. Somebody's serge dress of navy blue, **and** simple hat with just a suggestion of red in it, is not meant for the scrutiny of critical eye-glasses. She carries a satchel of sketching materials; while the Young Man, who is wonderfully juvenile this morning, bears the shepherd's crook that was once of good service to him in climbing Ben Nevis in the year of a memorable "border raid." And Sweetbriar, too, **is** of the party, with an animated flush on her **pale,** sensitive, poetical face at the anticipation of two whole days amid the moors. **I wonder who it was** who first called our little Hypatia "Sweetbriar"; but I can easily understand **why,** for **she** always carries such **a quiet aroma of** intellectual sweetness about her, impalpable but present, indefinable but irresistible. She makes such old-fashioned, fanciful, philosophical remarks with such childish faith, such sweet innocence, such perfect trust, as to lead one almost to wish she could never grow older **and know** what a hollow hypocritical humbug of a world it is into which **she** is **born.**

It is not a far cry from Buxton to Hayfield by train. Hayfield is the point for striking Kinderscout, the highest mountain in the Peake countrie. I dare say a good many people will smile at my ambitious vanity in describing this moorland height as a mountain at all; and no doubt it would appear even contemptible to the tourists who have found in Switzerland a telegraph office 6,000 feet above the sea, and have "cabled" direct away from the **Alps** to America. But one's estimation of hills should not be measured by the foot, like gas; any more than the beauty of a river should be regarded by the number of miles absorbed in its length; or the loveliness of a lake appraised by its largeness. Bigness is not always beauty. Diamonds are never found of great dimensions; and precious stones are not to be weighed by the pound avoirdupois. The latter observation comes from Sweetbriar, herself an illustration of the charm of little things.

Hayfield, says the Young Man as we arrive at that place, ought to be called Haguefield. The English tourist when he is at Antwerp hardly knows whether Antwerp was made for Rubens, or Rubens for Antwerp. Hayfield might have been made for the late Mr. Joseph Hague, who died at nine score, in 1786. He was one of the men who begin life with the traditional two and sixpence and attain to the opulency of Crœsus. Joseph Hague's first trading transactions were done as a pedlar with a few small articles in a basket. Then he bought a donkey, went to London, and became wealthy. Somebody asks with a laugh whether the ass in question had the same happy influence over his commercial destiny as a certain cat exercised over the fortunes of one Dick Whittington, sometime Lord Mayor of London? Certain it is that Joseph Hague became fabulously rich, and in the years of his retirement came to live near Hayfield, where he died. The Charities of Hayfield are his bequests. In the

Church there is a sonorous mural monument in marble, surmounted by a handsome bust, to his memory. This church—standing between the river Kinder and the stream from Phoside Valley—is neither ancient nor architecturally attractive: but the Young Man, who is well up in Cox's *Derbyshire Churches*, tells a good story about the Hague monument, as we leave the church behind and drive as far as the first of the Kinderscout passes. It appears that the beautiful monument was first erected in the neighbouring church of Glossop, where the good man it commemorates is buried. The chancel of that edifice was to be rebuilt, and the churchwardens were sorely exercised as to the removal of the Hague memorial to a place of safety. Fearful lest it should be stolen (it had cost £420), these sagacious Dogberrys placed it in—the lock-up. When thus "in durance vile," the occupancy of the cell was shared by a violent "drunk and disorderly," who, in a state of liquid lunacy, commenced a violent attack on the white and silent bust. The monument to this day bears marks of the disfigurement. So discreditable a transaction excited the indignation of one of the heirs of the Hague estate. The monument was at once taken out of custody, and erected in Hayfield Church, where it has received better treatment than it met with at Glossop. There is a strange sequel to this strange story, which is not without a tender touch of pathos. A few years ago an elderly stranger sought the parish clerk of Hayfield. He desired admission into the church to see the Hague monument. After gazing at the memorial with reverent earnestness for some time, he expressed his satisfaction at seeing it so well cared for. The verger, concluding that the visitor was connected with the family, told him of the ignominious incident in the lock-up. With tears in his voice, the stranger stopped the recital of the story. "Nobody knows "that better than myself" he said. "I was the "drunken man who knocked the monument about "in Glossop lock-up. I have since been abroad for "many years, and have only just returned to "England. The damage I did to that monument "has often troubled my conscience, and I determined "that as soon as I set foot in England again, I "would at once journey to Derbyshire to see what "had become of it; and now I am satisfied."

I have been regarding Sweetbriar's face while the Young Man has told the story, and what a revelation of deep interest was written there. It would have been a study for Leslie, a suggestion for Millais, a sketch for Sandys. We have left behind the grey, bleak, scattered stone houses, and the isolated print mills of Hayfield; and now, a mile or two only out of the town, the steep slopes of Kinderscout block the path against further riding. Walk we now must, for the burly mountain monarch will receive only the homage of the active and the hearty, the nimble-footed and the lusty-winded. The person who would find favour with the Kinder King must leave his crutch and toothpick, his patent leather boots and languid manners behind. There is no nonsense about this natural "Peveril of the Peak." Sturdy is he in his sympathies, and rough and rude and old-fashioned in his robust ways. It is the wish of Somebody to take the path to the waterfall which descends from the head of Kinder, the wild beauty of which she wants to throw upon her canvas. The Young Man and myself are somewhat imperiously informed that we may then potter about with our pipes. Sweetbriar holds views of ambitious breadth with regard to the *flora* of the mountain.

What a glorious walk it is to the Kinder Downfall. It seems incongruous, however, that we cannot explore the wild solitudes of the Scout without an "order." Fancy binding the Kinder King with red-tape, and applying "rules and regulations" to the broad freedom of the moors. This mountain, over which the pedestrian might have at one time roamed at his own sweet will, has become absorbed by the various proprietors of the adjoining lands. It is now strictly "preserved," and the tourist, cherishing an old-fashioned faith in the freedom of the mountains, is apt to come into ungrateful greeting with the keepers, if he is not armed with the official *open sesame*. The necessary "order" is, however, not difficult to obtain; and the Young Man tells me in this connection that the footpaths and bridle-roads of the district have aroused the interest of some neighbouring gentlemen who, under the name of "The Hayfield and Kinderscout Ancient Footpaths Association," endeavour to guard from further interference such footpaths and bridle-paths as belong by indisputable right to the people, and also to prevent, as far as possible, annoyance to legitimate landowners from the trespass of excursionists heedless of private rights in their reckless pursuit of pleasure. This second motive of the Society is a laudable one. Mr. W. Walker, the president,—a jealous guardian of the rights of the public, mark you,—tells us that he has witnessed many wanton depredations of well-meaning, but thoughtless persons. Once he saw a *mêlée* between Sunday-school teachers, who armed themselves with beautiful specimens of foxglove, torn from the bank side, and who in their pious ardour tore several yards of wall down; on another occasion a number of tourists, observing how steep a field was, proceeded to roll the coping-stones from the loose walls of the district to the peril of the sheep in the pasturage below; again, at the railway station, a tourist was innocently displaying his "find" during his ramble—only sixteen moor-birds' eggs!

While the Young Man has thus been **discoursing** in his usual discursive manner, we have gained the summit of Kinder Low, an eminence of 2,088 feet. The entranced eye skips over grey gritstone knoll and wild clough, lying immediately below, wine-stained in heather-bloom, and accentuated in outline in the white, cloudless light; passes the lonely white farm houses that here and there give a human interest to the spacious solitudes in the slopes of the valleys; lingers for a moment on the soft peaceful repose of Edale; and wanders over the map-like area of far-off peak and plain, now sharply defined in the strong sunshine, now dreamily indistinct in **the** impalpable silvery haze of heat. Right away **in** the south-west some hills that are sketched against the sky, like softly-tinted clouds, are the Welsh mountains; and beyond, Somebody's glasses search out for us the Irish Sea, a grey, glimmering plain, almost imperceptible against the remote horizon. The sun, picking out every tint of the moor, is tropical in its white glare above; but the wind blows a gale around us in delicious freshness. The Young Man's long grey beard is stirred like a sail;

Somebody's hair is blown in a wild tangle of sunny brown all over her face; Sweetbriar's ribbons flutter like the pennons of a yacht. The Young Man says Kinderscout in the winter time is as breezy as that American place where it takes four men to go for one walk: one to do the walking, the other three to hold him on his legs while he is doing it! Just below our eyrie is the Kinder Low Cavern, a hole which is not worth exploring by people who have seen Poole's Hole, at Buxton; the Blue John Mine, at Castleton; or the Rutland Cavern, at Matlock. So we press on through the heather northward. There is the somnolent hum of bees in the purple blush of the heather; now and again a moor-cock rises with a frightened cry; sometimes we make the acquaintance of an impudent black-faced sheep, who stares the ladies out of countenance with shameless effrontery; ever and anon Sweetbriar breaks away to make up a bouquet of silvery white-headed cotton sedges, ivy-leafed crowfoot, and blue-eyed forget-me-nots. The most striking feature in the rugged landscape now is the Three Knolls, a trinity of rounded hills rising from a deep hollow in close company; and then we are filled with speculations as to a ruin which is known to the Young Man as the Old Smithy. Come now the imposing Cluther Rocks, with a *debris* of time-stained

IN THE KINDERSCOUT COUNTRY.

millstones, strewn about in picturesque disorder. Presently we cross the little Redbrook, which is in a great hurry to run away from its bleak mountain home; and then lo! there is a musical roar in the air. Somebody utters a cry of delight, and we behold the smoke of the Kinder Downfall. Before The Twelfth brought the country such a burst of brilliant weather, there had been a serious spell of wet, and reports of floods filled the newspapers sufficiently deluged with the watery eloquence of St. Stephens. However unfortunate the excessive rain may have proved to the farmer, it has been flattering to us—if one can be so supremely selfish as to place one's own petty pleasure before the absorbing agricultural interests of an entire country—for it has given to the Kinder Downfall, which otherwise might have been dry, a volume of water which makes us simultaneously compare its power and beauty with the famous Falls of Foyers. Somebody has fixed her easel in the cool hollow looking direct up the great foaming gorge; and I wish I could reproduce in this cold column her vivid picture, which repeats the poetry of the scene in all the enchanting inspiration of its rugged outline and varied colour. The cataract descends from the lofty table-land at the head of Kinderscout, down an angle formed by two steep flanks of the mountain, and falls from ledge to ledge of the great black obstructing rocks in successive plunges of several hundred feet. It is at the lowest gorge, called the Runge, that Somebody's little patch of white canvas is to be seen. Looking up at the plunging water, she has spread before her a revelation of romantic beauty; the picturesque pushed to almost a theatrical point of possibility. The roar of the water fighting against the huge flanking rocks is the only sound. The sun catches the water, and now it is a dazzling constellation of diamonds; now there is a softer lambent light, as the shadow of an obtruding rock softens the glitter; then the spray is a beautiful prism; anon the smoke is a sunny mist broken into glints and splinters of light. A mountain ash here and there hangs its vivid coral berries over the headlong torrent; cool ferns show a tender green against the gritstone crags; lichens and mosses cushion the rocks in every shade of orange, and brown, and green, and yellow, and grey. The Young Man has found out a resting place on a couch of heather. He has unpacked a basket, that is now going to liberally reward us for so much trouble in the way of carriage. A bottle of dry champagne is placed in a cold pool to cool; in the meantime the Y.M., with a sparkle of humour in his eye, produces a well-remembered flask, and, pouring out a libation of "Arnbarrow," says, "Derbyshire scenery is best seen through a glass."

The tonic atmosphere has certainly stirred the **vagus-nerve.** Something less tempting **than the** present contents of the luncheon basket **would** have met with an alert appetite from all **four** of us. Even the etherial Sweetbriar confesses to a stomach; **and the** lady with the mahl-stick is not too æsthetic to be assisted to a little more of a certain game pie. We shall not readily forget that wild dinner **on the** banks of the Kinder. Trout rise to our crumbs, as we drop them on the water; once we catch sight of a kingfisher's rainbow breast; further down **the** stream—where a broken old mossy bridge "**makes** a hoary eyebrow for the gleam beyond it"—a melancholy heron stands in lonely vigil; the Young Man remembers years ago seeing the eagle on Kinderscout. We leave Somebody and her sister at the picture—be friendly to it, Sir Frederick the Great, with thy Council of Selection, when it comes in full view of thee and thy brother judges!—and crossing the little river, strike still in **a** northerly direction across the cliffs. Far away below the still water **of** a lonely tarn gleams in the sun. It is the Mermaid's Pool. Legend has lent to it a weird interest. Further on **we** come to a stupendous tumult of weather-beaten rocks, to which it seems ridiculous to bestow the domestic and little title of the "Armchair." But "Armchair," anyhow, suggests rest; and we seat ourselves here surrounded with the natural ampitheatre of Kinder. The view arrests conversation by its bold wildness and sublime solitude. We sit and smoke. In our tobacco trance we are more united in sympathy than if we chatted the closest confidences and made the most friendly mutual confessions. Speech would seem a profanation. The poetry of silence prevails. Its pathos is only broken by the distant echo of the sportsman's breechloader, and the plaintive call of the plover. The sun brings out a wonder of colour from the moorland vastness. There is the black of the swampy peat; the rose of the heather flowers; the grey of the coarse grasses on the boggy hillocks; the soft shade of the deep hollows. Suggestions of silver and gold are given by scattered wild flowers, gorse, and lichens. Down below, the windows of a lonely farmhouse laugh with sunlight, and there is a vivid green patch of meadow where the hay has been newly gathered. In the far distance there is a pearly grey where the moor mingles with the sky at the hazy horizon line. The moors have often been compared to the sea; and the vast breadth of undulating distance at Kinderscout gives special force to the trite fancy. It is an ocean of billowy heather; distant hills rise like dark sea cliffs; a far-off ordnance survey cairn supplies the illusion of a lighthouse; here and there a block of dark gritstone, growing above the purple waves, with the sun catching on its weather-stained side, conveys the suggestion of a russet sail; a remote farm looks like an island in the heathery sea.

The afternoon wears on and still we are Lotos Eaters. We might have "sworn an oath," and mean to

"Keep it with an equal mind,
In the hollow Lotos Land to live and lie reclined
On the hills, like Gods together, careless of mankind."

The stillness and solitude, the infinite space and the lofty remoteness of these towering ridges above the littleness of the work-day world, come as a satisfying solace to soul and sense; an ineffable charm to the eye, a deep peace to the mind, a sweet contentment and calm to troubled nerves and harassed life. This love of the hills is really a sacred thing. It is a religion. The Man of Sorrows went up into a mountain to pray. The world below becomes but a babbling booth of little lives, small ambitions, and sordid ideals; and he who can pass a day on the heights without coming down the better in mind and soul is not to be envied.

There is a blitheness and buoyancy in the air that stirs us at last into a further walk. Our talk is of how much the dweller in towns appreciates the country.

> "*Only those who in sad cities dwell*
> *Are of the green trees fully sensible;*
> *To them the silver bells of twinkling streams*
> *Seem brighter than an angel's laugh in dreams,*"

I poetically protest. Pretty, but generally inapplicable argues the Young Man. The strength of habit, he maintains, prevails over the spell of the hills, and he instances Doctor Johnson, who, when asked to spend a day in the country, replied in his usual "bow-wow" manner, "Sir, I hate green fields. One green field is exactly like another green field. Sir, let us take a walk down Fleet Street;" and Charles Lamb, who, when asked how he had enjoyed the lakes and mountains of Cumberland and Westmoreland, answered that he was obliged to think of the ham-and-beef shop near St. Martin's Lane! Some people take London with them wherever they go; and a highland shooting box is every bit as Sybaritic as a Piccadilly Club. The charm of the moors is destroyed when Pall Mall is thus taken into Perthshire, and the sophistries of a complex civilisation break upon the simplicity and solitude of the heather. This, mark you, is only a small portion of the Y.M's. profound observations on the subject. He is still inveighing against the laxity and luxury of the present age when we arrive at the north-western point of the Edge. A large cairn here marks the second highest point of the Peak range: 1,981 feet. When we had gained the ordnance barrow on Kinder Low we were at the greatest altitude: an eminence of 2,088 feet. The table land is flat and boggy, and furrowed with deep water courses, that expose the mountain gritstone beneath. The waters are shed west and east, the Kin and Sett entering the Goyt and the Mersey, and the Ashop and and Noe flowing east to the Derwent. While the western side of Kinder appeals to the artistic eye as strongly as any Derbyshire scene of which I know, there is a fascination in the Ashop side of the mountain. The Ashop waterfall is as wildly beautiful as the Kinder downfall. The river, as in the other instance, flows from the great trackless table land. There is a savage gorge of gloomy precipitous rocks, strewn with mossy boulders, through which the bright brown peat-stained water flashes and foams till it reaches its leap, which is through dark weird rocks that form a rude arch over the plunging fall. The river now descends in its picturesque headlong course in an easterly direction, keeping along the northern flank of the Scout. Here it is

fed by tributary streams from the swampy moors
and mountain ridges. After winding for some three
miles it falls in love with the Lady Brook, and the
two healthy joyous streams skip hand in hand
through a narrow defile close by the Sheffield and
Glossop road. It would be pleasant to pursue the
Ashop and Lady Brook along their romantic route,
past the pretty "bit" of water-colour where the
Alport becomes their sweet-faced child, and right
away through the Woodlands, beautiful with birch
trees, to Ashopton itself. Following the "Edge" to
Fairbrook Naze, we step down briskly to the Snake
Inn: a lonely hostelry shining white in a belt of
dark firs. The "Cat and Fiddle," near Buxton,
claims to be the house of the most elevated enter-
tainment in the kingdom; but the traveller should
get the real "mountain dew" at the "Snake," which
is 1,069 feet above the sea. Shenstone found his
warmest welcome at an Inn; but I doubt whether
the poet had such scenery thrown in as the "Snake"
affords from its hospitable doors. Behind are the
tors of Alport moor; right opposite are reared the
sturdy shoulders of Fairbrook Naze, one of the
boldest ridges in the whole of the Scout; while the
jagged, fantastic cliffs known as Seal Edge afford a
wild romance of rock. The Young Man has some-
thing to say about the turnpike in front of the door.

This Glossop road, he tells us, is no engineering trifle. It is, he believes, unsurpassed in height by any other turnpike in England, scoring, as it does, 1,666 feet amid the morose moorland. The heather encroaches on either side of the road; at intervals there are tall poles to guide the traveller in time of snow. The Dukes of Devonshire and Norfolk are credited with the construction of this emphatic highway.

It is a lonely walk of several miles back to the locality of the Kinder Downfall. The two artists must have now lost their light for the picture. There is a flush of red and gold in the west; and the hilly ridges are growing dark in the deepening shadows, save where some remote peak is brought strangely near and distinct in the warm colours of the sunset. But the Young Man, bless you, has no concern for the girls. We are to find them, he says, at a certain isolated farm in the great breadth of valley under the Kinder Fall, at which house a smoking hospitable meal awaits us. A confusion of hay ricks, of grey gables, of thatched roofs of lichened russet, and of tiled roofs of finely-toned red. A square, solid, low-spreading stone house, with thick walls as abiding as the gritstone crags to which they once belonged. This is our good caravansary. A chained mastiff gives us a fierce salute as we approach the gate; but Somebody and Sweetbriar, thus apprised of our arrival, change the turbulent fury of the wild animal into quite a frisky friendliness, into much wagging of tail, clanging of chain, and bounding of joy. Over the hills in the west there comes a strange melodramatic radiance of blood red, which fades impalpably into a tinted mist of rose and amber; while in the south the scarcely risen moon is striking silvery and cold over swelling ribs of dark heath; in the sky overhead is a clear twilight; at present the stars do not show. There is the babble of an adjacent beck; there is the soft coo of pigeons somewhere up in the shadowy mossy roofs of the farm building; the cattle are being driven in from the pasturage to be milked; the plover is calling "pee-wit-pee-wit" on the moors; we can hear the muffled roar of the Kinder Fall. This is the only house within a radius of some miles.

The girls seem quite familiar with the interior. Somebody is showing off her art in the mashing of tea, singing all the while in her soft contralto voice:

"*Oh the oak, and the ash, and the bonny ivy tree,*
They grow so green in the North Countrie."

What a broad fine specimen of the Peak farmer our host is; but I wish he had not grasped my hand with quite such a fervid grip; still one shouldn't wear rings. And what a quaint grace there is about his good wife, as genuine and shining as the old polished oak chairs and tables of the room. And the room itself, with that black old oak furniture, **which would** fetch any price in æsthetic Kensington; and with a great fire-place as big as the drawing-room of a modern villa, and under which one can sit on an old oak settle in the ingle-nook and **see** the stars. And the heartiness of our evening meal, with the inviting milk that drinks like cream, **and** which induces one of us, who comes from a great town, to wish he could have the rich beverage **laid** on in pipes at his house, in a supply as plentiful as the water. The Young Man has on his knee two bonny, brown-faced, bright-eyed children with a tangle of hair that makes them look as shaggy as Shetland ponies. **He** is singing

"*Ride a cock horse to Banbury Cross,*
To see a fine lady on a white horse,
With rings on her fingers, and bells on her toes,
She shall have music wherever she goes."

Each of the Y. M's knees is a wild "cock horse," going at a sensational trot, while the young riders cling on and crow with delight. The old gentleman who is thus unbending was a friend of Count D'Orsay's, and the fingers of the clock of time must be put back a few hours, I fancy, to recall those days.

After tea we saunter in the cool air outside. All around is the **majesty** and mystery of the moors by moonlight; the weirdness and wonder of the mountains at night. The twilight has cleared away; and the moon has climbed above the hill, and sheds a broad path of silver down the slope of the moor, so strange and etherial that Sweetbriar says it seems to be a road of light for us to walk up to the gateway of Heaven. Kinderscout is a heavy mass of hill rising sheer and dark like a wall up to the stars. The planets, throbbing in the great silent wold of sky, seem very near to us. The Evening Star, in the rarefied air, is as lustrous as the Koh-i-noor. The pole star is like a lighthouse gleam in the north; faint and far-off is the diamond dust of the Milky Way. In the east Mars pulsates with a ruddy light; there is the radiance of Jupiter. Between these two great planets, the intense pure white light of Vesta is to be seen in the clear serenity of the sky; while that bluish-white light, seldom revealed to the naked eye, is Uranus. Sirius is the brightest star in the whole sky. The Pleiades stand out among a world of stars; there is the V shaped cluster of the Hyades. Sharply defined is King Charles's Wain; Orion wears a silver belt; the jewels flash in Cassiopeia's chair; there is the pale wistful gleam of Andromeda's face; and there are other trembling white constellations, each of which Sweetbriar connects with some classic romance. Once or twice a shooting star flashes across the sky. And now the moon is rising more overhead of us, as we are walking alone in this silent, solemn world of moorland masses, with the weird Scout rising like **the** apparition of another sphere. The road shows white in front of us. Somebody is talking in quite a Ruskin manner about the **blackness** of the shadows that impart so much mystery into the picture, and the sharpness of the light that searches out both **colour and** outline. **The** Young Man explains that the thin purity **of** the air gives strength to the starlight. Sweetbriar is enchanted with the scene. The moonlight falls with a softened radiance on her sweet young face, and invests it with a saintly fancy. The moon seems to belong entirely to this Derbyshire **moor**land, and to be shining alone on our own sympathetic little group. It seems strange to **think** that there is a world outside these hills, **and that the** same placid face is looking down upon **many** countries and upon millions of people at this very hour; upon London's teeming streets, upon the lighted chattering Boulevards of Paris, upon the water ways of Venice, upon the laurels of Italy, upon great ships outward and homeward bound in mid-Atlantic. And what scenes other than this simple healthful undulation of the Peake countrie the same moon surveys with the

K

same impassive gaze: scenes of love and hatred; of **hope** and **despair**; of success and failure; of joy and **fear**; **of** reckless sin **and silent** self-sacrifice; **of debauchery** and devotion. The **same impenetrable eyes look on** the squander of riches **and the squalor of poverty; on** mental wrestlings and moral prostrations; **on pale** sick chambers and **gay** ball-rooms; on **the dinner party** given by Mr. Crœsus, M.P., **the special event of** the season, and the lonely stone cell where a murderer can hear the fixing **of the** hideous apparatus that shall make him dangle a dishonoured corpse at eight o'clock prompt **in the morning; on** mothers in quiet country-side villages, **praying** for sons exposed to the temptations of great cities; **on** women selling their souls in **infamy; on students at** midnight lamps; on the burglar stealing forth on his mission of plunder; on humour and pathos; **on** laughter **and tears; on** the endless tragedy and **comedy of** human **life; on** carnival and charnel **house**; on the weeping eyes and shrunken face of Melpomene, and the inane laugh of Momus; **on** swaddling clothes and winding sheets; **on** hopes that are broken and ideals that **are shattered; on** friendships that are faithless and loves that are **false.** The moon regards all these contrasts—the good **and** the evil—with the same placid face. She **is moved neither** to love nor pity.

She has seen the same scenes and contrasts in the world for these thousands of years, and may be she will see them for thousands of years to come. She is the same moon whose argent light shone on Homer's Camp before Troy; and gave such romance to Lorenzo's wooing of Jessica; and revealed the sleeping Endymion. The same moon whose beams lit up the hoary, haunted ruins of the Colosseum for Byron, and inspired Ben Jonson's deathless lyric. The pale Empress of Night, with her retinue of stars, is destined to look down on many battlefields yet, to affect generations of lovers yet unborn, and to inspire whole libraries of poetry. The one dominating feeling of this communion with the solemn starlit moors is, indeed, a revelation of the eternal and immutable. Human existence seems a frivolous, fleeting trifle compared with the unchanging moon, and stars, and hills that have seen the generations come and go. The mind is stunned with the sense of its own smallness; and——

It is very cruel of the Young Man to upset us with a spirit of flippant levity, to associate Luna with lunacy, and to say to the moon

"*Never you mind: shine on.*"

But, perhaps, the Young Man is as affected by the emotion of the hour as any of us. Can I remember sufficiently well a masterly passage in the *Strange*

Adventures of a Phaeton to quote it accurately:—

"It is no wonder that lovers love the starlight, and the infinite variety and beauty and silence of the strange darkness. But folks who have got beyond that period do not care so much to meet the mystery of the solemnity of the night. They may have experiences they would rather not recall. Who can tell what bitterness and grevious heart-wringing are associated with the wonderful peace and majesty of the throbbing midnight sky? The strong man, with all his strength fled from him, has gone out in his utter misery, and cried, 'Oh God, save my wife to me!' And the young mother, with her heart breaking, has looked up into the great abyss, and cried 'Oh God, give me back my baby!' and all the answer they have had was the silence of the winds and the faint and distant glimmer of the stars. They do not care to meet the gaze of those sad, and calm, and impenetrable eyes."

It is, however, growing chilly. The moon is bringing out the red roofs and grey gables of the farm in sharp silhouette; there are yellow lights in the window for us. What a picture for a shadow-loving artist—for a Rembrandt, a Schkalken, or a Doré—is the broad, low room in which we are seated. A bottle of whisky finds its way on the table, also a quaint iron tobacco jar; peat is smoking in the old-fashioned fireplace, over which is suspended a three-legged iron pot; and the strange smell of the turf makes us think that we are somewhere up in Sutherlandshire. There is an old lamp, which compensates in power of perfume what it lacks in clearness of illumination. But the light suits the room just as an artist would adjust it. Glow and gloom seem to alternate. The shadows are broad, and warm, and mellow. The light catches the old oak chairs; there are weird shadows thrown across the ceiling, half revealing and half hiding an old fowling piece, a string of onions, and some hams enclosed in white bags, suspended from the rafters; ever and anon some copper vessel flashes in the luxurious semi-darkness; mysterious reflections flicker on the wall; the red glow falls upon the old clock case, and upon shining dish-covers that might have been cunningly arranged in order to concoct a Dutch painter's "bits" of light and shade and "doubling of line." A collie blinks before the fire; the odour of the peat is exquisite. The Young Man, with his fine face profiled in the uncertain light, and a yellow tinge spreading over his long grey beard, reminds me of the King of Borva. Somebody, with her simple manners and natural grace, suggests Princess Shiela. Frank Lavendar is not in the group. It is difficult to think that we are not somewhere up in Scotland; but we are at least in Derbyshire. "If North Wales is not Switzerland, it is none the less North Wales," is one of the wise sayings of Charles Kingsley.

The Young Man is engaged in a deep conversation on yonder shadowy settle, open to the sky, with a flaxen-haired philosopher of the advanced age of seven.

"Now, what should you like to be, Joseph?" we hear the Y. M. earnestly ask. "A lawyer?"

A shy shake of the head.

"A doctor?"

A shake of the head, with a shudder.

"A clergyman?"

"No!" emphatically.

"Perhaps you would like to be a soldier now, a captain, you know, with a sword?"

"No! I should like to be a butcher."

"A butcher! Why? Oh why?"

"*Cos their 'osses goes the fastest.*"

It is time for Joseph to go to bed. Indeed, he has been specially privileged in regard to remaining up to-night. He retires, after marvellous draughts of new milk. Somebody and the good wife are very confidential. Our host is discussing with the Y. M., slowly and deliberately, the question of the bygone allotment of the land to various adjoining owners. "Luke at Kinder"—he says with much honest indignation—"while the rich mon has received according to his riches 2,000 acres, the poor mon has not bin geen a single yaerd o' land. In fact, the poor hae been robbed on the 40 acres o' what used to be knowed as t' Poor Mon's Pace (piece), and oe'r which t' poor o' 'Ayfield 'ad the rights o' turfery. But t' ole plot 'as bin absorbed in proivate estates."

"Fairfield Common will be claimed next," says Sweetbriar, with the mournful air of Cassandra prophesying evil of her beloved Troy. No wonder that so robust a religionist as Mr. Spurgeon is incensed at this modern spirit of selfish exclusiveness, and that we find him writing: " I sometimes " feel very glad when I look at the sea, and think " that it belongs to the great and generous God, and " not to greedy man. Here upon land every foot of " earth is enclosed by somebody, and jealously " guarded from trespass. The village had a breezy " common, upon which a poor man might at least " keep a goose; but the great folks could never rest " till every inch was put within hedges and made " their own. You can scarcely walk anywhere with- " out being met by ' *Trespassers Beware*.' Mountains " and hills, which everybody ought to be allowed to

"climb without leave, are fenced in and kept free
"from all intruders. . . . No such greed can
"appropriate the sea. The free sea cannot be
"parcelled out, nor hedged, nor ditched, nor dyked,
"nor walled. It has no lords of the manor, but
"remains free and unappropriated for ever." Such
grasping Conservatism is enough to make us Radicals, or Communists, or Land Leaguers, or something
equally wrong and revolutionary. I wonder, by the
way, if the red Phrygian Cap of Liberty would suit
Somebody as well as the Blue colours she wore at the
last General Election? It certainly makes a very
charming *chapeau* in M. Jean Gautherin's marble
impersonification of " The Republic."

To put an end to the grievance the Y. M. proposes
a song. After a little pressing, the farmer rolls out
the old strains of " The Vicar of Bray " in a hearty
baritone voice. Later on, Somebody is persuaded
to attempt a song without accompaniment. We
have never heard it before, and the air she imparts
to the sweet homely Scotch pathos is her own.

> *The bairnies cuddle doon at nicht,*
>   *Wi' muckle faucht an' din;*
> *O, try and sleep, ye waukrife rogues,*
>   *Your faither's comin' in.*
> *They never heed a word I speak;*
>   *I try to gie a froon,*
> *But aye I hap them up, an' cry,*
>   *" O, bairnies, cuddle doon."*

Wee Jamie wi' the curly heid—
　He aye sleeps next the wa',
Bangs up an' cries, "I want a piece"—
　The rascal starts them a'.
I rin an' fetch them pieces, drinks,
　They stop awee the soun',
Then draw the blankets up an' cry,
　"Noo, weanies cuddle doon."

But ere five minutes gang, wee Rab
　Cries oot, frae 'neath the claes,
"Mither, mak' Tam gie ower at ance,
　He's kittlin' wi' his taes."
The mischief's in that Tam for tricks,
　He'd bother **half** the toon;
But aye I hap them up an' cry,
　"O, bairnies, cuddle doon."

At length they hear their faither's fit,
　An', as he steeks the door,
They turn their faces to the wa',
　While Tam pretends to snore.
"Hae a' the weans been gude?" he asks,
　As he pits aff his shoon.
"The bairnies, John, are in their beds,
　An' lang since cuddled doon."

An' just afore we bed oorsel's,
　We look at oor wee lambs;
Tam has his airm roun' wee Rab's **neck**,
　An' Rab his airm roun' Tam's.
I lift wee Jamie up the bed,
　An' **as** I straik each croon,
I whisper, till my heart fills up,
　"O, bairnies cuddle doon."

The bairnies cuddle doon at nicht
　Wi' mirth that's dear to me;
But sune the big warl's cark an' care
　Will quaten doon their glee.

> Yet, come what will to ilka ane,
>   May He who sits aboon
> Aye whisper, though their pows be bauld,
>   "O, bairnies, cuddle doon."

This piece is surely worthy of Robert Burns at his best, and that was certainly when he was most simple and domestic in his lay. It is, we discover, by Alexander Anderson, a platelayer on a Scottish line of rails. . . The hour is late, for the country, and urges that we, too, should "cuddle doon." The girls retire; but our host stays up to smoke with us an ultimate pipe and drain an ultimate glass. We are loath to leave the room; the flickering lights would enchant an artist. There are trembling reflections in every shadowy corner; the face of the Y. M. stands out of an ebony background, like the study of "a head" in an ancient picture; while the lamp casts an alarming silhouette of the farmer's head and shoulders on the wall behind.

What a great ghostly old bedroom the Young Man and myself share; a room big enough to run a steeplechase in over the widely divided furniture. And what a great ghostly old bed; an antiquated four-poster, heavily canopied and curtained, in which one could get lost; a bed almost as big as its overrated contemporary at Ware. But there is a pleasant smell of lavender about the sheets, and the Young Man is already snoring like a trombone in trouble.

The moon peeps in weirdly through the lattice windows. Once an owl flutters past with a hoot. There is a scramble of mice in the wainscot. A clock in the room ticks with a thrilling, throbbing emphasis. The room seems full of corners, and each corner boasts a closet, with great brass handles on the doors. It is just the room for ghosts. I believe I should see a ghost were it not for the Y. M's solo on the nasal trombone. It has been the dream of my life to see a real respectable good-mannered ghost. Speaking of dreams— . .

The Young Man shakes me roughly in the early dawn and bids me rise and see the sunrise. He is already dressed and humming

"*As I was going to Darby, Sir,*
 All on a market day,
 I met the finest Ram, Sir,
 That ever was fed on hay.
 Daddle-i-day, daddle-i-day,
 Fal-de-ral, fal-de-ral, daddle-i-day.

I wish he wasn't quite so vivacious. I am an old young man; he is a young old man; and the balance of spirits seems all in favour of the latter. I am supremely sleepy. The strong mountain air is more somnolent than poppies; the long walks of yesterday have made me stiff and tired.

"Get up, my boy, at once," continues the Y.M., with a voice of command, trolling

> "*The Jaws that were in his head, Sir,*
>   *They were so fine and thin,*
> *They were sold to a Methodist Parson,*
>   *For a pulpit to preach in.*
> *Daddle-i-day, &c.*"

"Just one more minute," I implore, with an effort. He goes trampling down the broad echoing stairs; I hear the sound of life stirring in the yard; there is a confusion of farm voices, and after that I am steeped in sweet sleep. . . . The Young Man, with an assumption of temper, breaks in upon my rest, hours after, to say that breakfast is waiting. I never saw the sunrise, of course. If I had only been left alone I might have got up just in time to see it set; like Mark Twain who, when up the Rigi, missed the *morning* horn-blow at the Rigi-Kulu hotel, and saw the rare spectacle of an evening sunrise. Readers of *A Tramp Abroad* will recall this critical incident in the life of the American humourist. . . . I suppose the sight of the sun coming up over the bleak misty shoulders of Kinderscout was a spectacle to be remembered. I am rather glad I missed it, for I should have lost the girls' enthusiastic description of it: how there was a cloudy wall of dark mountain edged with a cold grey light; how that became a saffron, which warmed to a pale rose and sent up lances of light, spreading in the shape of a fan; how everything which had been hitherto blurred, indistinct and spongy, slowly emerged from its misty monotone, and showed delicacy, sharpness, colour, and detail; **how** the sun itself—a blood-red shield—floated above the topmost ridges, and swam higher and higher in a bath of **gold,** till the whole heavens caught the glamour and glory of a new day.

The chief sensation at breakfast is the appearance of the young philosopher Joseph, drenched through. He has fallen into the forbidden horse-trough in the yard. Soaked is he to the skin. The Y. M. is severe.

"Now suppose you had been drowned and had gone straight to God, what would He have said to you?" he enquires.

"He'd a sed you'r very wet."

There is really no reasoning with such a boy; and the Y. M. takes his revenge by flying a kite with the culprit's brother. In China the old men only are allowed the pastime of kite flying. How would it be to call the Y. M. the "Heathen Chinee?"

We get back to the Kinder Fall. Somebody must have another hour or two at her picture. **It is** another day white with heat; but there is a brisk stir of wind which gives movement and light and shade to the panorama. Pleasant it is to sit and watch the cloud-shadows sail in soft progress over the hills, pursued by tidal-waves of strong sunlight that bring out every gradation of colour, garnishing the gold of the furze, warming the purple acres of heather, picking out the green of the bracken, and showing the sharp, shining greys of far-off rocky ridges.

After luncheon our farming friends, who have business at Castleton, drive us thither by rocky devious roads, along the soft, sylvan Edale Valley, by Mam Tor, and through the Winnats. At Castleton we catch one of the big excursion breaks which ply between there and Buxton, and avail ourselves of the homeward journey of the vehicle. One side of the break is ornamented by Young Manchester, a dozen callow youths, slangy, shallow, sallow, whose "loud" get-up is emphasised by their vulgar manners. The other row is composed of young couples who swoon on each others' shoulders and encircle each others' waists. The Manchester line is spirituous, and sings, amid the fume of much cheap cigar, "Dear old pals, charming old pals." The opposing rank of Joseph James'; and Maria Eliza Hannahs', is spiritual, and is singing in debased tune: "We shall meet on that beautiful shore," with quite vehement and unnecessary certainty. The effect is striking—very striking. Our companions are to us as the offensive unaspirated Cockney bagmen were to Christopher North on that memorable journey by the Dumfries mail-coach from Edinboro' to Tweedside. Luckily the Y. M. obtained seats for the girls on the box, with one of the jolliest reminiscences of the old coaching times that exists in these days of cads and paper collars.

The summer day is fast declining as we approach our journey's end. The sunset is shining over the wild western ridges of the Peak. The hills seem to soar larger in the burning crimsons and purples and golds of the glowing sky. As the conflagration of colour spreads in splendour, our Philistine cargo is silenced by its magic and wealth and wonder. The beauty of the scene increases

"Till all the sordid earth
Is hued like Heaven, and Life's dull prison house
Turns to a golden palace."

The sun itself has now sunk behind the hilly ridges, giving to their broken edges an embroidery of fire. The sky cools from the radiance of flaming reds and crimsons and carmines into delicate gradations of orange and amber; but the hills facing the sunset still reflect the glow; a solitary chimney, set here and there on a steep slope, becomes idealised and shines like an Eastern minaret, while the gables of a lonely house are magnified to twice their actual height. The light dies; the day is done; and now the infinite tranquility of a clear twilight comes over hill and valley; and the peace and beauty of it possesses us until it is broken by the life and movement of Buxton, stirring after the drowsy heat of a tropical afternoon.

There is not much more to be said concerning our two days' desertion of duty. All that does remain Somebody begs to be allowed to offer. And surely the readers whom I have rendered most irascible by my intolerable prolixity will listen to her brief postscript. She says:—

"I am *very vexed* to think that you have associated my *poor little* picture of the Kinder Downfall with Sir Frederick Leighton and the Royal Academy. It will *never* leave Derbyshire. It is *already* given away, and when I have made it *less imperfect* it will go to Mrs. ——, of —— Farm, near Kinder, in memory of " Cuddle Doon."

ROUND AND ABOUT BUXTON.

"*Buxtona, quæ calidæ celebrabere nomine lymphæ,
Forte mihi posthac non adeunda, vale.*"
—MARY QUEEN OF SCOTS.

I forget what was the nervous affection—was it rheumatism or neuralgia, sciatica or gout?—which led to my residence at Buxton for two or three months some time ago, "when this old cap was new." It could not have been gout, for I was too poor to afford the pleasure of such patrician pain; but whatever the ailment was I left it behind me at Buxton. I wished I could have also left behind me a large donation—at least a thousand pounds—to the funds of the Devonshire Hospital, as a thank-offering to the gracious virtues of St. Ann. But I had more gratitude than gold. "Poor devils of authors" are rich only in regrets. Brewers and butchers, publicans and provision-merchants, people who fill your belly, instead of your brain, are most able to write out that "leetle cheque" which I should have liked to have enclosed to Doctor Robertson. Liquor before literature; beefsteaks before books. Do you remember the wealthy miller in George Eliot's story who "didn't think much of education," because he felt himself in a position "to buy up most of the educated men he knew?" I have always admired that pregnant passage of John Ruskin's, which I am pleased to observe a famous firm of publishers have prefixed to their list of books. He writes:—

"I say we have despised literature; what do we, "as a nation, care about books? How much do "you think we spend altogether on our libraries, "public or private, as compared with what we spend "on our horses. If a man spends lavishly on his "library, you call him mad—a bibliomaniac. But "you never call one a horse-maniac, though men "ruin themselves every day by their horses, and "and you do not hear of people ruining themselves "by their books. Or, to go lower still, how much "do you think the contents of the book-shelves "of the United Kingdom, public and private, would "fetch, as compared with the contents of its wine- "cellars? What position would its expenditure on "literature take as compared with its expenditure "on luxurious eating? We talk of food for the

"mind, as of food for the body: now, a good book
contains such food inexhaustible: it is provision
for life, and for the best part of us; yet how long
most people would look at the best book before
they would give the price of a large turbot for
it! Though there have been men who have
pinched their stomachs and bared their backs to
buy a book, whose libraries were cheaper to them,
I think, in the end, than most men's dinners are.
We are few of us put to such a trial; and more
the pity; for, indeed, a precious thing is all the
more precious to us if it has been won by work
or economy; and if public libraries were half as
costly as public dinners, or books cost the tenth
part of what bracelets do, even foolish men and
women might sometimes suspect there was good
in reading as well as in munching and sparkling;
whereas the very cheapness of literature is making
even wiser people forget that if a book is worth
reading it is worth buying."

Since those early Buxton days, however, I have realised a little mammon by one or two shares in the Megatherium Mashtub and Thames Stout Company, sufficient to induce me to establish my only son, James Adolphus, in the malt trade. "There's millions in it," as the American play says. Doctor Johnson, when taking stock, as executor under

Thrale's will, of the old brewery which was to be known to another thirsty generation as Barclay and Perkins's, told Topham Beauclerck that he had at last discovered the "source of boundless prosperity and inexhaustible riches." A splendid career awaits James Adolphus. The mashtub will make him a modern Midas and an M.P. He will give a Temperance Hall and a Working Men's Intellectual Institute to his native town; become knighted; and bequeath, together with many thousand pounds sterling, the real respectable hereditary gout to his children. He and they will no doubt give according to their gout and gold to the Devonshire Hospital, which brings me back to Buxton, from whence I ought not to have strayed.

I was anxious to remark, ere the demon of digression took possession of my pen, that when staying at Buxton those two or three months, I met the "oldest inhabitant," and he could give me a fresh walk to a fresh place every day. Not long tiring trips, mark you; but short easy strolls, and every morning a new walk. My friend has done more, perhaps, for Buxton, more for her progress and public improvements than any man, or any body of men, in the neighbourhood. He has been the Haussmann of the Peak. We—that is a small coterie of congenial spirits who know something of the delights of the *noctes cænæque deorum*, knighted him out of respect, "Sir John." He isn't "Sir" John, save for the hearty heraldry of friendship; but he ought to be. There are, on the other hand, a great number of Sir Johns' who oughtn't to be; so matters are thus balanced. I have a rough diary of one or two of the "tiny travels" that Sir John took me in those days, mere strolls to arouse the *fames endeudi*, or evening saunters before turning in for whist. That diary started with the very best intentions of presenting a full and faithful record of the year; but it fell off considerably from its early promise, as most diaries do. What a barren history for instance is this: "May 9th, warm natural bath (2s.) at St. Ann's at eight; breakfast at nine (ham and eggs and coffee); lunch at one (chicken not tender); dinner at six. Fifty sat down, which is rather good for the Old Hall for May. Fine day; but could not get the *Times*." Here is another entry on a subsequent page: "May 29th. Bought bath ticket this morning at shop under Colonnade." Speaking of the sale of bath tickets, Sir John tells us a good story of a Lancashire lad and his lass coming one Whit Monday into the same shop. "Wiggin," "Bowton," and "Blegburn," are masters of the situation at Buxton at Whitsuntide. They used to repair to Southport at this holiday season, until the sea retired in disgust before their ardent addresses; and now a mournful steam-tram pier, which seems to stretch half-way to America, must be traversed before you can catch sight of the waves. The Mr. "Bowton" of the story came into the dainty Colonnade shop. He was decorated with a necktie that resembled in its discordancy of hue an inebriated rainbow. His *amorata* stood awkwardly behind in a festive shawl and bonnet whose colours were sufficiently "warm" to justify the instant calling out of the local Fire Brigade.

Quoth the elegant Mr. "Bowton." "Oi wants a beth tickit."

"A lady's or a gentleman's?" is the polite enquiry from behind the counter, seeing that the applicant is accompanied by a "lady."

An awkward pause.

"Is it a gentleman's ticket you require, sir?"

"Noä. It's for mä."

But I am rambling without progressing. I think I mentioned that Sir John found me a fresh walk every day. We generally met in the Gardens. He took such an interest in the birds that he could summon round him by a low whistle all the ducks, the water-hens, the Chinese geese, the coot, the swan, and what not, off the water from a considerable distance. The peacock, too, would come and peer wistfully for **Indian** corn **from his** coat pocket ; **the** trout would receive broken bread from his open palm ; and as for the glossy pigeons **I have** seen their pretty pink feet alight all over him, perch on his hat, fight **for a** place on **his** shoulder, and stand in rows along his outstretched arms. The Buxton pigeons are the plumpest, prettiest, most prosperous **birds I know. They always** remind me of the Pigeons **of** St. **Mark at** Venice, that hover **about the bronze well in the** courtyard of the Piazza. I have never been to Venice, or beheld **St.** Mark's, **or** lingered **in the** Piazza ; but still the Buxton birds remind me of their Venetian cousins ; just as the Devonshire Dart, **or** the Monmouthshire Wye, recalls the romantic Rhine to people who have never visited the Fatherland. I think I said Sir John found me **a fresh** walk every day.

The Corbar Woods, **I** mind **me, was one of** the first spots to which **I was** introduced. Dear green old Corbar ! First impressions go **a long way** and last a long **time** ; and my early experience of the deep peace, the secluded **beauty, and** the picturesque charm of Corbar is only endorsed by each subsequent visit. The wooded slope was, **I** thought, very **steep** and sheer that morning, in the early summer **time,** when first I clomb its sides ; but **I** was anxious to "**get up in** the world" then ; and what an ample reward of far-stretching scenery did the wind-swept summit bestow. Now I can find easy serpentine paths under the labyrinth of leaves, and rustic seats at intervals, where I can sit and listen to the tuneful whisperings of the tremulous trees. Sir John did not take the spirit of romance out of Corbar when he told me that these plantations are laid over the remains of an old gritstone quarry, which give the rugged gorges that add to the wild charm of the place. Corbar seems to have been invented by Pan himself specially for lovers. Those narrow winding walks beneath Gothic arches of green, with leaves of lambent light above, shedding a tracery of chequered shadow on the grass below, are just the paths for whispered confidences and confessions; for protests and promises; for youth and hope and love and dreams. The foliage this early summer time is unbudding; there is a gentle hesitancy as to colour; in other trees there is that first translucent tint of delicate green, as transient as it is tender. The undergrowth is thick with uncurling ferns, and is starred with primroses and forget-me-nots. The latter might have sprung up in graceful compliment to the romantic young people—Phillidas and Corydons—that haunt the place. But I notice among the forget-me-nots the yew tree. What does that sombre growth in this sacred trysting place? Ah, my brethren, the cypress comes quite as often as the orange blossom in the history of young hearts; and that yew tree, I doubt not, could—like Tennyson's "Talking Oak"—be eloquent of dreams that are dissolved and ideals that are shattered, of broken pledges, dead hopes, and the sad "might have beens." Corbar has seen all the loyalty of love, and the courage of constany, no doubt, "when girls were girls and hearts were hearts;" but it has beheld the joke of the jilt, and the fatal flippancy of the flirt, and witnessed Lady Clara Vere De Vere "break a heart for pastime, ere she went to town." The Saviour of Mankind was betrayed by a kiss; and many of his disciples have been since.

Leave we Armida's Garden, Celia's Arbour, and the fateful Bower of Proserpine, for another of Sir John's short strolls. Solomon's Temple! A place you would naturally associate with oriental magnificence, with wealth and wisdom, and the beautiful Queen of Sheba. But, as Mr. Longfellow remarks, "things are not what they seem." There is plenty of the "east" about Solomon's Temple, but it is the "east wind;" and the bare mountain ridge overlooks miles of wild moss and moor, and the shoulders of bleak, misty; hungry hills. Still it is a lovable spot for all that, and seems to bid you come and climb its easy eminence and breathe the fluent blue air that bathes its head. We are sure to meet and chat with two or three pleasant people we know as we pass along the Broad Walk. Having run this social blockade, we take the path through the fields which brings us to Grin Low, softly shaded with dark pine and fir. It is grateful to saunter with pipe and a novel of James Payn's through these deep wooded paths, to rest on a felled tree, or a couch of rock cushioned with moss. The shade of pine and fir makes a "dim religious light;" straight red columnar trunks suggest cathedral pillars; the branches arch in retreating avenues; there is a roof of green, with patches of blue sky for window-panes; ever and anon the tremor of the wind is as the soft music of a far-off choir.

A huge mass of stones on the top of the massy hill, once forming a rude tower, is called Solomon's Temple. The title is, of course, a ridiculous one. It owes its origin, Sir John says, to the cairn having been erected when the land was occupied by one "Solomon" Mycock. Hence "Solomon's Temple," applied with a caustic relish peculiar to the tart yeomen of the Peak. The view from the eminence of the Peaks of Axe Edge, Kinderscout, Mam Tor, Lord's Seat, and Chelmorton Low, is a dream of wild scenery; while the thin buoyant air acts upon brain and nerve with instantaneous zest. "Op'n thee mahth, Meary; op'n thee mahth, an' get aw't' air tha con!" is the advice attributed to be given by a poor woman to her daughter in these parts; and Solomon's Temple is just the place for such a lung bath.

Another walk, far less known than the others I have indicated, Sir John once took me in May time. Threading the Serpentine Grounds, we then struck along a path across the undulation of meadow land that divides the Manchester and Burbage Roads. A white farm-house shines amid a gloomy belt of firs on the hill right in front, known as Watford. Past this farm, and by the side of the steep wood beyond, from which you can see Buxton lying white and radiant in the sun, locked in with the encroaching hills. One is in no hurry to leave the sylvan seclusion of that deep old wood, fragrant with fresh resinous odours. The lullaby of leaves is music to the weary mind and the jaded nerve. The gentle wind stirs a harp of pines, and it responds in a sweetly sympathetic strain. The sun is warm overhead; there is the trill of birds in the branches; all around is the scent and colour of wild-flowers. Turn your head which way you will there is a green glade, a woody vista, ready made for the artist. The walk is through a long lonely country road, called Bishop's Lane, since a by-gone Colonial bishop once lived in yon house close by, that is smothered in trees. And it is one of the most deviously pretty lanes in the Peak. Hawthorn trees line the path. Now they are in full white flower. The air is heavy with their sweet intoxication. Just an ideal lane; a lane to loiter in and listen to the birds, and pick up wild-flowers, and imagine you are young again.

> "The primrose takes a deeper hue,
> The dewy grass a greener look;
> The violet wears a deeper blue,
> A lighter music leads the brook."

I am very sorry when the lane leads me out on to the dusty highroad against Burbage Church, about a mile from Buxton. Suppose we return the same way. Come hawthorn fragrance! come again deep bowery wood!

There is no place I can call to instant memory which is more immediately surrounded with "beauty spots" than Buxton. It is the key to a hundred picturesque places; the threshold of ever so many scenic charms; the centre of a number of natural attractions. Belted with forest, wooded walks are afforded in every direction. What a charming "bit" of wood that is leading out of Ashwood Dale on the left, and climbing, thickly carpeted with wild-flowers, up to Pig Tor. Here is a view worth coming many miles to behold. You look sheer down from this limestone scar on five distinct converging vales: a startling *coup d'œil* in landscape of exquisite beauty. Close by here is Deep Dale, another favourite *petit pelerinage* of Sir John's. Deep Dale branches off the Ashwood Dale road on the opposite side and near to Pig Tor. It is a deep, treeless, lifeless valley, whose opposing sides dip sheer into the path that winds at the bottom. Rugged and romantic throughout, two or three curious caverns, without the inevitable "guide," add to its attractions. I have walked along its riven sides several times and never met a human being. A capital carriage drive might be made through it without much expense. . . . Here you can gain access to Sterndale, a glorious wooded walk, knee-deep in ferns and flowers. Few visitors in Buxton ever discover it, yet it is close at hand, steeped in poetry, a lyric of leafy loveliness. . . . There are walks, too, round Fairfield not to be despised. Seen under certain lights—the golden mellowness of an October sunset, or the red tinted mist of a December afternoon—the undulating common assumes a strange grey vastness and sense of distance, that only a Turner, with his trick of atmospheric glamour, and power of aërial perspective, could hope to produce. I remember it in the tempestuous twilight of a Christmas afternoon, when I had been skating on the pond there. Fog was struggling with frost; the plain then appeared like a vast and billowy sea, whose waves were breaking over a faint line of weird light reflected in the eastern edge of the far horizon. The shadowy church seemed like a spectral beacon tower; the white-washed houses on the edge of the common became phantom fishermen's huts on the sounding beach. In the grey dimness was a yellow speck of light that might have been a ship's lamp. Everything was in mysterious shadow. I never saw a more suggestive, subdued, sad landscape. But for strange atmospheric effects let me commend you, Mr. Cobalt Blue, to the "Cat and Fiddle" on the moors round Axe Edge. It is about six miles from Buxton, this lonely hostelry among the hills; but there is a somewhat shorter cut by the lower road, which has the added charm of a savage wilderness. You often get a sea of pearly cloud below you, shrouding in soft fleeces of white many a mountain cone, rounded knoll, and pointed peak, while the sky is blue and bright above. It is pleasant to walk out to these western moors in the waning sunset light, and to see the fading fire sink again and again behind the hilly ridges to re-appear as soon as you gain their summits, thus giving you a succession of sunsets and sunrises; and then as you turn back and see the moon rising over the yellow lights of Buxton, a mere hint of a town in the hollow, the return journey is full of artistic charm. The "Cat" is just one **mile in** Cheshire; so it is a Cheshire **cat,** and grins **in** the most approved Cheshire **cat style.** The "**Cat**" stands low-spreading and four-square against the winds. No wider or wilder moors could surround a human dwelling. Hills rise above hills; rocks oppose rocks; moors mingle in moors. There are valleys within valleys: hollows hide hollows. The prevailing tint is grey; but in the conflagration of a stormy sunset there is a study of intense tints—a spread **of** fiery splendour—that the boldest artist would hesitate to attempt. . . . Sir Walter Scott, by the **way, places** the "Cat and Fiddle" miles away from its site. The author of the "Peveril of the Peak" never was in the Peak, and it is difficult to trace Castleton at all by his description of the place. But no matter. The northern Ariosto, in dealing with his own country, made of Roseneath an island. It is consoling to know that "Homer sometimes nods," since it allows the humble scribbler to take **his** "forty winks."

Poole's cavern, perhaps, hardly belongs to "Undiscovered Derbyshire." The cheap-tripper is its greatest patron; but it is, indeed, worthy of more intellectual visitors. Sometime ago, the present writer was staying at a little hostelry in Millers' Dale, with Christopher Kenrick, the popular novelist, better known as the "King of Bohemia." His gifted artistic daughter was stealing away each day on her sympathetic canvas (to take away to the great city) such cool suggestive glimpses of rock and river, hidden clough and hanging cliff, dreamy "bits" of water-wheel and little studies of cottage life. His scientific son was out among the ravines with his geological hammer, and coming in laden with so much indifferent building material, which he turned over with the gentle love which one might spend upon sapphires and diamonds. A chip of old millstone grit gave him a feverish felicity; a genuine bit of Blue John was as a foretaste of heaven; while an atom of dirty bitumen was bliss ineffable. Handsome Mrs. Christopher Kenrick, was, I think, pining for Piccadilly Circus; for the cooking at our inn was not the most dainty, and there was another drawback to our delight. It was a picturesque spot. But angels have faults, and there was one discordant note in the sweet harmony of Millers' Dale, one bar sinister in the glorious heraldry, one blot upon the pretty picture, one disfiguring cloud in the bright sunshine, one bitter flavour in the way of our happiness. Bang! Bang! Bang! and a noise of falling rock that reverberates like sullen thunder. They are at it again those utilitarian limestone quarrying men. They are despoiling the grand old cliff opposite, robbing **the hills of** their Alpine beauty. **All day long** the bombardment continues. All day long there is the smoke from the lime-kilns. Night brings **no** cessation of the din. One can surely **now** appreciate John Ruskin's righteous **wrath against** all these Limestone Quarry Companies (Limited) who are defrauding the scenery of its greatest charm, tearing the graceful rocks in twain, and filling the air with smoke and explosion. If you want to see Millers' Dale, come **at** once, before it is gone. It **is perilous now** to venture up to Chee Dale by **the Wye** side. A new quarrying Company have commenced operations in the midst of Arcadia itself, and a warning in white paint on a black board tells you of the danger of proceeding **up the** river path. Millers' Dale **will soon be destroyed**, its sylvan seclusion murdered. **Topley** Pike **is** being reduced day by day to something closely resembling a rammel heap. Where will these despoilers stop? Chee Tor, now, contains many cubic feet of magnificent limestone. **So** does the High Tor **at** Matlock **Bath.** Fortunately, Mam Tor at Castleton is not limestone; but Pickering Tor at Dove Dale would prove **a** lucrative "working." The next

M

generation will, peradventure, see these old glories of our Derbyshire Dales measured out for destruction. Their names, perhaps, will soon become a mere tradition. Oh, yes, it is good for trade I grant you, gentlemen, and Capital is power. Peg away, Mr. Gradgrind. Yes, Sir, Facts, Sir. Away with sentiment. Sentiment is, of course, a mistake. Hurry up your trucks, Mr. Alderman Cute. These "tors" must be "put down." It is all for the good of the country; and are we not a "nation of shopkeepers?"

It was, I remark, a picturesque spot. I revive the picture. A weedy old waterwheel mixed up among the trees on the banks of the Wye, just where a landscape painter would have placed it. Limestone cliffs rise from the water in a curve of grey and green. The little reckless river, which has just slipped from the cold restraint of its stony-hearted father Axe Edge at Buxton, is running away to sea, like a truant schoolboy, as fast as it can past weeping trees and obstructing rocks. Everything outside is fresh and green. The trees wear their first tender bridal sheen of green. There are spring flowers on the river margin. A blue moth sails past like a hare-bell with wings. The flowers in the tangled bank are like butterflies; the butterflies are like flowers. A mayfly came sailing into the room just now. It came in with a breeze that had just kissed the swathes of new mown hay. A river keeper in velveteens drops in to gossip about the trout, and to tell us how the hard winter had killed the fish. He says the melted snow from the mountains afflicted them with a strange disease. They sickened and died, and the speckled beauties were brought up from the river-bed in buckets full.

The river shines through the trees. Its music comes through the open window. Sun and shadow change the valley into a thousand different pictures during the day. In the early morning, Christopher Kenrick and myself find a secluded pool by a moss-grown bridge that invites us to plunge into the heart of its cool depths.

" Those brilliant sunny mornings when we tumbled out of bed,
And hurried on a few rough clothes, and to the river sped!
What laughing joyaunce hung about those merry days agone,
We clove the rushing torrent at the early flush of dawn!
' Tremendous headers' took we in the waters bright and clear,
And splashed and dashed, and dived and swam, just off old Blankton Weir.

. . . .

Was ever indolence so sweet, were ever days so fine,
As when we lounged in that old punt and played with rod and line?
'Tis true few fish we caught there, but the good old ale we quaffed,

*As we chatted, too, and smoked there, and idled, dreamed,
    and laughed:*
Then thought we only of to-day, of morrow had no fear,
*For sorrow scarce had tinged the stream, that flowed
    through Blankton Weir.*

. . . .

And I mind me of one even, so calm and clear and bright,
*What songs we sang—whose voices rang—that lovely
    summer night.*
*Where are the hearty voices now who trolled these good
    old lays?*
And where the silvery laughter that rang in bygone days?
*Come back, that night of long ago! Come back, the
    moonlight clear!*
*When hearts beat light, and eyes were bright, about old
    Blankton Weir."*

But touching Poole's Hole. Sir John found us out and we were inveigled over to Buxton. Christopher Kenrick insisted on seeing Poole's Hole. It was his first visit to this really grotesque geological miracle. Pending the arrival of that ship of mine, which has been so long overdue, and which has so frequently been delayed by the "trade-winds," and so often "sprung a leak," I should not object to rent a cavern like this Poole's Hole. It must be quite a mine of wealth to Mr. Redfern, who rents the interesting excavation from the Duke of Devonshire. Men may come, and men may go, but the sixpences come to Mr. Redfern's turnstile for ever. Outside the Hole are some tea-garden trumperies,—white figure-heads of ships from Liverpool, and two-penny-half-penny horrors in statuary—whose precise connection with geology it would be difficult to determine. But the whole is good change for the entrance fee. There is a curious Museum of odd, out of-the-way prints and pictures, and a collection of fossils, coins, and relics of the Stone Age, the Roman Occupation, and the Saxon Period, dug up from one time to another in the cavern by Mr. Redfern, who is an intelligent curator. The latter are suggestive commentaries upon history. They make a reflective man think. What a rush of history occurs when you pick up that little stone lamp, which once, perhaps, lit a Roman maiden to bed, but which was extinguished for ever, before the birth of Christ! And what are your speculations, my friend, as you look with curious eye upon that jaw of white shining masculine teeth, imbedded in that piece of limestone rock? Here are human bones of all periods and ages. Sir John violates our reverie by profanely suggesting what a confusion of bones there will be at the Last Day when those labelled limbs upon which scientists now speculate, will be rushing to find their companions in osteology, and that skullery of heads will start off in search of the missing trunks. There is some black old furniture, too, dating back some hundreds of years. Here is the original Old Grandfather's Clock still going, "tick, tack, tick, tack," although it is three hundred years since its rude wheels were first set in motion. Here moreover, is an old bedstead, ancient enough to be the bed of Procrustes. A heavy over-hanging canopy is suspended over the head, like the threatening sword of Damocles. A date of the sixteenth century is carved on the bed, together with grinning cartoon faces that are enough to frighten you out of your sleep by their Satanic leer. Here, too, is an old oak desk, whose worm-eaten drawers must have contained many an old family secret, and enshrined many a sturdy yeoman's "last will and testament."

But the greatest curiosity Mr. Redfern produces is the guide. I hate guides. They ought to be suppressed by Act of Parliament. They render Matlock miserable, and make Castleton a cruelty. But there are guides everywhere and guides there always have been. Mark Twain insists that "within "a hundred years after Adam left Eden, the guide "probably gave the usual general flourish with his "hand and said: 'Place where the animals were "named, ladies and gentlemen; place where the "tree of the forbidden fruit stood; exact spot where "Adam and Eve first met; and here, ladies and "gentlemen, adorned and hallowed by the names and "addresses of three generations of tourists, we have the "crumbling remains of Cain's altar—fine old ruin!'"

But stay! our Guide is waiting to escort us to the Cavern. Button up your coat, I beg of you. How cold it is! We seem to have stepped at once from the torrid zone to the glacial mean. The *cicerone* is a small boy with a big voice. A fierce *falsetto* voice. The basest treble voice I ever heard.

"Whose Hole is this?" asks Christopher Kenrick with solemn curiosity.

"Poole's Hole," says the small boy.

"Fool's Hole?" remarks Christopher gravely.

"*Poole's* Hole," exclaims the big voice pitched to a shriek.

"Ah, yes, Poole's Hole. His 'den,' in fact. Is it Mr. Poole, the author of *Paul Pry;* or Mr. Poole, the tailor of Saville Row? Are you Mr. Poole's son, my boy?"

The juvenile stares.

"Where is Mr. Poole? Is he at home?"

Another stare that reaches over the boy's face and spreads itself all over Buxton.

"Is he dead?" asks our friend sorrowfully.

"Yes, mony a year. He wor a bandit, 'undreds o' years ago."

"What did he die of?"

"Dunno."

"'Derbyshire throat,' maybe?"

This banter was continued until the Small Boy

gave Christopher Kenrick over as a monster of crass ignorance. Then we proceeded to explore the weird darkness and spectral formations of the curious cavern, with its Rembrandt-like shadows and Dante horrors. But the demon of unbelieving levity had been aroused in Christopher Kenrick's bosom, and would not be still. The guide began the description which I had heard a dozen times before. He gave it without the variation of a word, or the change of a gesture. He showed us stalactites and stalagmites, encrinites and ammonites.

"Have you any Adullamites? They hide themselves in caves," said Christopher Kenrick in a voice of innocent enquiry.

"Here are some," said the boy, pointing out a cluster of fossils that bore no flattering likeness to Mr. Lowe and Mr. Horsman: that "party of two," which bore so striking a resemblance to the young lady's terrier, "which was so covered with hair that you could not tell which was the head and which was the tail of it," to quote John Bright's irresistible description.

"Here you will see the resemblance to a dome," said the shrill voice, as its owner pointed a species of lamplighter's stick to the wet roof.

"Where? I cannot see it," said C. K., earnestly.

"There!" responded the boy with furious emphasis,

astonished at finding his oft-repeated descriptions for once challenged. The most excruciatingly ridiculous names have been bestowed upon the stalactite and stalagmite petrifications. "Here you see the resemblance to a poached egg." Again we objected to the comparison. We could not discern the similitude. A serious crisis was reached when we stopped at another winding in the wet vault, and the little boy with the large voice turned on a jet of economical gas, and said:

"Here you see the resemblance to the hind part of an elephant."

Christopher Kenrick adjusted his eye-glass and scrutinised the petrification critically.

"No, my boy, this will not do. You are too rude. Trot the animal round and show us his tusks. You are positively indecent."

Presently came "Mary Queen of Scots' Pillar."

"What was that?" asked Mr. Kenrick, as if he had missed an important announcement.

The guide repeated the description.

"And what"—indignantly—"did Mary, Queen of Scots, do here, boy?"

"She came to Buxton to get cured of rheumatism."

"Yes, yes. We know all about that," Christopher Kenrick rejoined. "But what was this Queen's particular business with regard to this pillar?"

"She leaned agen it, sur."

"Leaned against that damp, dirty stone! Impossible! Did she wear a mackintosh? Perhaps not. How imprudent. She might well have rheumatism."

The boy regarded it as a really serious question. But we could not preserve our gravity any longer; and when next the shrill voice announced:

"Here you see the resemblance, &c.," Christopher Kenrick put his hand in his pocket, and imitating the boy's falsetto voice, said:

"Here you see a remarkable resemblance to a shilling;" and the juvenile Troglodyte at once saw the likeness, and as he pocketed the coin, we left the cavern and entered the waves of warm air outside, now apparently parched as the atmosphere of a Turkish bath.

The dark rushing water that lends such poetic horror to Poole's Cavern is the River Wye. Its baby life is one of trouble. It only runs away from the grim Axe Edge, to get lost in the mysterious gloom of this great cavern. Nearly frightened to death, it escapes from this gruesome vault to be tortured in the Buxton Gardens into unnatural leaps and windings. The dirty coal-measures of Burbage then take the shining colour from its young face, and daub it with a sickly ochre. Then it is inveigled under the town of Buxton through slimy holes where sewage poison takes away its health. Strange that it should outlive all this ill-treatment to make of Millers' Dale a romance, and of Monsal Dale a dream, where one could almost sigh for the revival of the classic days, so that one might turn river-god, or naiad, to revel in the crystal current as it makes music under the crags, and mirrors fern and foliage and flower bending low and lovingly to see their reflected beauty in its liquid light.

CHATSWORTH

AS A

TREASURE-HOUSE OF ART.

" Chatsworth! thy stately mansion and the pride
Of thy domain, strange contrast do present
To house and home in many a craggy rent
Of the wild Peak; where new-born waters glide
Through fields whose thrifty occupants abide
As in a dear and chosen banishment,
With every semblance of entire content."
WORDSWORTH.

I am, for this day only, the Guide to Chatsworth. My service to you, ladies and gentlemen. This way, if you please. Did I conduct the readers of *The Magazine of Art* through the palace of the Peak corporally, instead of in the spirit, I am afraid my ill-trained voice would only reach a few of the foremost fringe of the good people pressing to see the art-treasures of the palace. Indeed, the great house itself would hardly hold the throng, which would spread over the green acres of the glorious park, and cause the General Manager of the Midland Railway Company to run a special service of trains to Rowsley station, the threshold of Chatsworth. But, donning the cap of Fortunio, and assuming the stilts of Asmodeus, I ask you to follow me invisibly. It shall be my endeavour to repay the honour by being as unguide-like a guide as possible, neither repeating cut-and-dried descriptions, like a parrot with a mechanical memory, nor bursting forth at inopportune moments with inapposite quotations of unpunctuated poetry. But here are the keys, and I present you my service again; together with a welcome to Chatsworth in the name of His Grace the Duke of Devonshire, K.G., whose liberal spirit fences the place round with no selfish exclusiveness, but throws open both park and palace so freely that one is like a public picnic-ground, and the other is more suggestive of a popular museum than a princely mansion.

One or two of our party are loitering behind among the green glories of the park, I see. We must forgive them for lingering among such leafy loveliness. However poetical may be the landscapes that brighten the walls of Chatsworth, none can be so fascinating as the pictures framed by the gilded windows of the house. Vignettes, these of wood and water, rock and river—the soft acres of the park, with the fallow deer wandering among the soothing shadows of gnarled old trees; the dark wooded masses of hill flanking the ducal mansion, topped with a wind-swept shooting-tower; the Derwent gliding through the wide meadows fronting the house, the river here showing white and broken water over a weir, there shining in still pools under overhanging branches; the House itself starting with fluted columns from the bosom of the scene, a stately mass of beautiful buff stone, which the tinting hand of time has toned down to an harmonious cream colour that contrasts with the green gloom of the forest foliage behind; the Peak country climbing up to the sky in the picturesque perspective. "How old is the present house?" Well, the existing mansion only dates from the latter half of the seventeenth century, being built by that William Cavendish, Earl of Devonshire, who played so heroic a part in the Revolution of 1688, and who retired to Chatsworth from an historic criminal information and employed his time—as Lord Macaulay phrases it—"in turning the old Gothic mansion of his family into an edifice worthy of Palladio." "His magnificence," says the same historian, "his taste, his talents, his classic learning, his high spirit, and the urbanity of his manners, were admitted by his enemies." Chatsworth House is, indeed, the monument of that munificent nobleman. He scarcely survived the **completion of** the palatial pile twelve months. Dr. White Kennett, the Bishop of Peterborough, in preaching the funeral discourse of the departed Duke, said the prodigious expense incurred in the structure of the building was the least expense "if regard be made to his gardens, waterworks, statues, pictures, and other the finest pieces **of art** and nature that could be obtained abroad or **at** home." The Duke appears to have engaged the best contemporary artists **of the** day in the embellishment of his Derbyshire mansion. The classic allegories on wall and ceiling are the conceits of such painters as Verrio, Laguerre, Sir James Thornhill, Richard Highmore, Price, and Huyd. The chief worker in iron **was M.** Tijou, whose daughter **was** the wife of Laguerre. The carving was divided between Cibber, Watson, M. Nadould, Geeraerslius, Harris, Nost, Davies, M. Auriol, Lobb, and Lans**croon.** William Talman and Sir Christopher Wren were the architects. William Cavendish's successors have enlarged the building, and enhanced decade by decade its art-glories. The northern wing was erected by the late Duke. Some of you may, perhaps, contend that the architectural *tout-ensemble* of the Ionic façade is not improved by the addition. The house is like a body with only one arm. A wing on the other side is wanted to give the building completeness and perfect repose. The old house was one of the prisons of Mary, Queen of Scots. The captive princess was then in the custody of the Earl of Shrewsbury. In the park there is a sombre bower, with a moat, which is linked with her name and misfortunes. As, however, there is scarcely an ancestral seat in the kingdom but what is said to have served as a place of durance for the northern queen, her association with Chatsworth has no particular charm. More interesting, you will think, is the testimony of another illustrious prisoner which relates to the present pile. The captive was Marshall Tallard, who submitted to the Duke of Marlborough at Blenheim. He was kept a prisoner in England for some years, and spent a short time at Chatsworth. The compliment he paid the reigning Duke, when he left his hospitalities, was worthy of a Frenchman. "My Lord Duke," he said, "when I compute the days of my captivity in England, I shall leave out those I have passed at Chatsworth."

If it please you, we will now enter the house itself. The entrance hall is not a chamber of imposing proportions, nor does a stately staircase meet the view over which you can work yourselves up into raptures. The ceiling glows with a copy of Guido's "Aurora," the work of Miss Curzon. That is a statue of Domitian; these are busts of Homer, Jupiter, Ariadne, Socrates, and Caracalla. A corridor with floor of inlaid marble gives access to the great hall, a truly noble apartment extending the entire length of the eastern side of the quadrangle. The floor **is of black** and white and veined marble, **artistic in design,** and exquisite in polish. There is much that is interesting in this superb hall. Inspect the immense marble table **in the centre of the** room. It is of Derbyshire marble, as also is the massive chimney-piece. The tablet surrounding the fireplace gives in a sentence the history of Chatsworth House. The inscription is in tedious Latin; but the translation reads, "These well-beloved ancestral halls begun in the year of English Freedom 1688, William Spencer, Duke of Devonshire, inherited **in 1814,** and completed in the **year of Sorrow** 1840." The "year of sorrow" **is** an allusion **to** the death of the much-loved and lamented wife **of the** present Duke. The walls and ceilings of this spacious chamber are enriched by Laguerre **and Verrio,** in a series of vast paintings illustrative of episodes in the life of Julius Cæsar, with colossal characters, like the prodigious Peters and **Pauls** that Sir James Thornhill **(whose work** we shall presently meet) painted suspended in a basket two or three hundred feet high in the dizzy dome of St. Paul's, or standing

N

on a frail platform up in the empyrean, covering with classic gods areas of ceiling and staircase greater than the Flemish ells of theatrical scene-painters.* There are bronzes, and other objects of artistic interest, in this grand hall, and on the exterior are some notable stone carvings in alto-relievo by Watson.

Leaving the hall, and passing down a corridor containing some cabinet pictures, Swiss views, and an exterior by Hogarth, the chapel is before us. Here all that painting, sculpture, and carving can do to enrich a room with artistic beauty has been elaborately employed. The sacred room is fragrant with the smell of cedar-wood with which the walls are wainscoted, and of which the reading-desk is

---

* "In or out of our Royal Academy, we have not a single painter sufficiently acquainted with the geometrical canons of foreshortening and concave perspective to paint a ceiling. Those canons are clearly and explicitly laid down in scores of books published in the seventeenth and eighteenth centuries; but those books find no English students. We console ourselves for our impotence by repeating Pope's pert sneer about the sprawling saints of Verrio and Laguerre, and by preparing to scrub out Sir James Thornhill's paintings from the dome of St. Paul's. We choose, in our complacent ignorance, to forget that the grandest achievement of pictorial art in the whole world is the painted ceiling of the Sistine Chapel in the Vatican." — *George Augustus Sala: "Paris Herself Again." Vol. I., Page 99.*

composed. The floor is of black and white marble in mosaic work. The altar is made of the finest Derbyshire spars and **marbles**, with sculptured figures of Faith and Hope, the work of Caius Gabriel Cibber, the father of the laureate-poet. The same sculptor executed the celebrated figures of "Madness" and "Melancholy" over the gates of Bedlam, which his son **Colley** refers to as "the brazen, **brainless** brothers." There are exquisite sculpturings round the altar, and ornamental wood-carvings by Grinling Gibbons, more of whose skilful work we shall soon encounter. The fine painting over the altar of "The Incredulity of St. Thomas" is Laguerre's. The same artist, together with Verrio, has filled the upper walls **and** ceiling with Scriptural scenes. As we leave the room pause to look at the wood-carving over the door of Cupids with musical instruments, with the entwined vase **of** flowers and foliage.

Now the house is all before us where to choose. I need not be tediously topographical in describing the position of the various suites of apartments, nor need we go over them in any classified order. Sketches before pictures. Let us visit the sketch gallery. It contains the largest private collection of original studies **by** old Masters in existence. **The** collection was amassed by the second **Duke**, the nucleus being secured at a great outlay at Rotterdam.

dam. The gallery comprises two large apartments, and the walls are completely covered with original sketches, divided into departments — the French, German, Dutch, Bolognese, Florentine, Venetian, and Roman schools. The collection is so exhaustively comprehensive that to merely mention the names of the contributors would be to give a catalogue of all the old Masters. These interesting drawings, some of them the initial experiments in sepia, pencil, or crayon, of great masterpieces, demand a whole day's thoughtful inspection; but they must be dismissed in a few minutes. Still note, I beg of you, the spirited studies of figures by Michael Angelo. They were for the ceiling of the Sistine Chapel. There is a head of the Virgin by Leonardo da Vinci. Raffaelle's pencil contributes the sketch for the picture by Pinturicchio at Sienna of "Æneas Silvius kissing the foot of Pope Eugenius IV. at the Council of Basle," the figure of St. Paul for the cartoon of the "Sacrifice at Lystra," the original sketch for "St. Catherine" (the picture now in our National Gallery), "The Virgin and Child," "Joseph discovering himself to his Brethren," and several others. Holbein is represented by such examples as his "Fall of Phaeton," "The Last Judgment," "Hagar and Ishmael," and "Diana and Actæon." Look, too, at the excellent specimens by Albert Dürer, Rubens, Rembrandt, Titian, Claude, Vandyke, Salvator Rosa, and Correggio, the study of which is an art-education. Adjoining the sketch gallery, and really part of it, considerable space is devoted to a choice collection of coloured paintings of birds. The artist is not known, but his acquaintance with the feathered tribe was large and minute, for every species of bird is presented, and the drawing and colouring are most meritorious in their fidelity and spirit.

Proceeding now to the state rooms, pause we at the entrance for a moment to admire the collection of specimens of ceramic art, represented by English and foreign makers, and then to behold the striking vista of the superb series of the state apartments, which occupies the whole length of the building. The first room in this splendid suite is the dressing-room. The floor, as in all the rooms before us, is of polished oak parqueterie, in which the light is reflected as in a mirror. The door-cases are of carved marble. It would be difficult for the most constrained and prosaic of persons, for the coldest professor of the *nil admirari* school, to describe the state apartments at Chatsworth without falling into the language of superlatives. One requires the ruby adjectives that glitter in Ouida's or Lothair's "jewelly hæmorrhage of words" to express his sensations. The coved ceiling is adorned in the centre with a painting of the flight of **Mercury on his mission to Paris, and on the coving are groups** depictive of the arts and sciences. But the most attractive feature is the wood-carving. Wood-carving, indeed, may be said to be the distinguishing characteristic of **Chatsworth**. It is *sui generis*, **and none but itself can furnish its own parallel.** Here is Grinling Gibbons' masterpiece. Horace Walpole has described it. It is a group comprising **a cravat of point-lace, a woodcock, pendent leaves and flowers, and a medal with a bust in relief.** Exquisite in its delicate clearness is the lace, while bird and foliage are wrought with a skill that makes the work indeed a *chef-d'œuvre*. It has been disputed whether the carving in question really is the work of Gibbons. More than one authority attributes it to the genius of Samuel Watson, a Derbyshire craftsman, who, **with** Thomas Young, William Davies, and Joel Lobb, **shared** with Gibbons much of the wood-carving at Chatsworth. Over the doorway is another group of carving, excellent in design and execution, representing a collection of carvers' tools—globe, compass, brace **and bit, square,** augers, chisels, gouges, together with a bust. On the west side of the room are several pendants and a group; and before passing on note that clever picture in mosaic, those artistic

Japanese cabinets, and the curious specimens of old earthenware. Come we now to the old state bed-room. More sights for the curious. Aurora chases away Night in the coved ceiling in great splendour of colour. Embossed leather of rich arabesque pattern, heavily gilt, covers the walls. The wood-carving again calls for admiration. There are cabinets, vases, and old beakers that would gladden the soul of a virtuoso; and there is a particularly interesting model of the tomb of Madame Langlan, at Hildebank, near Berne, in which the spirits of the mother and her child are seen bursting the barrier of their grave. This bed-room has no bed. But no matter. There is a noble state chair with ancient embroidery, marvellously worked by a countess whose fingers now are dust; together with the coronation chairs and foot-stools of George III. and Queen Charlotte, of William IV. and Queen Adelaide, and—shade of Sartor Resartus! —the wardrobe of Louis XVI. The state music-room: more wood-carving, more mythological gods sprawling in allegorical clouds on more coved ceiling, more embossed leather walls, this time relieved by blue. Here is the vigorously painted portrait of the first Duke of Devonshire, which is attributed to Vansomer. But the special object of interest in this room is a clever piece of painted delusion, executed on one of the double doors leading to the gallery. It is a fiddle painted with such *vraisemblance* on the door that, in the subdued light of the half-closed door, it has all the appearance of a violin hanging upon a peg. Everybody at first sight concludes it is a rare old fiddle, a priceless Stradivarius, one of the treasures of the place. Everybody is taken in by the happy forgery, just as everybody is duped by the deceptive paintings in the Museum at Brussels, from the morbid yet marvellous brush of Wiertz. Some people must touch—like Thomas the incredulous disciple—before they can be brought to believe. The tradition is that the fiddle was painted by Verrio to deceive Gibbons, who, in one of his carvings, had deceived Verrio. How anecdotes of art repeat themselves. Century endorses century. Did not Apelles induce a horse to neigh in recognition of the steed he had drawn? Did not Zeuxis imitate fruit so closely that the birds came and pecked at his painted grapes; and was he not himself deceived by thinking the painted curtain of Parrhasius real? Another exquisite carving is a feather by Watson. It is as light as swansdown. A gentle zephyr, you might almost think, would ruffle the hard wood.

Here we are in the state drawing-room. The walls are hung with Gobelin's tapestry from the cartoons of Raffaelle, representing Jupiter and Antiope with the Muses on Parnassus. Phaeton is driving the horses of the sun across the ceiling with much spirit. The principal wood-carving is a military trophy. The sumptuousness of the appointments in this room gives one a sense of overpowering splendour on the brain. The furniture is richly carved and gilt. There is old china that would drive an ordinary collector wild with envy. There are cabinets of ebony and ormolu of great beauty. Behold, in addition, this table of sea-green. It is of pure malachite, rarest of minerals, and is the largest in the world. Look, too, at this table of polished black marble inlaid with a mosaic of various coloured marbles, forming a wreath of flowers—lilies of the valley, convolvuluses, wild roses, blue-bells. The effect on the black ground is charming. Here is a copy of the Venus de Medici in marble displayed in the centre of a round ottoman. In the state dining-room, which next awaits your inspection, the ceiling is done by Verrio. It is a conception in classic allegory of the Fates cutting the thread of life, and is regarded by competent critics as one of the best paintings of the kind. There is an *embarrass de richesse* of choice wood-carving that almost palls upon one by its profusion. Do not let me hurry you through this apartment. Look at the fragile delicacy of the festoons of flowers in the panelling of the wainscoted walls; turn your attention to the doorways: over that doorway a group of leaves and corn, over the other two entrances groups of crabs, lobsters, fish, and shells. Then admire we the fireplace. Framing that octagonal tablet is the triumph of the wood-carver's art. It is a study of dead game. The summit is crowned with heron, pheasants, **grouse**, and other birds. Over these the net of the snarer is dexterously thrown. This, hanging down **the** sides of the tablet, forms festoons on which suspend snipe, quails, partridges, and pheasants. Each **bird** is a **picture.** Feathered wing and soft plumage are produced with a fidelity to nature which bewilders the spectator by its absolute perfection. Yes, I should say that this is no doubt wrought by the crafty hand of Grinling Gibbons, although the criticasters, who would deprive Shakespeare of the authorship of "Hamlet," **and** would **persuade** we puzzled Philistines that the statues of Praxiteles were done by vicarious **assistants,** are of opinion that the work was shared by the other carvers in **wood** to whom I referred a few minutes ago. Did not Horace Walpole write: "There is no evidence of a man before Gibbons who gave to wood the loose and airy lightness of flowers, and chained together the various productions of the elements with a free disorder natural to each species?" The busts in this room are by Chantrey and Nollekens of the Emperor Nicholas of Russia and his Consort, Fox, Canning, the Duke of Bedford, and others. On the central table is the rosary of Henry VIII., together with ivory carvings, silver filigree, and antique bronzes. There is a clock in pure malachite, the gift of the late Emperor Nicholas, and a charming marble model of the Victoria Regia. Carved marble doorways give access to the grand staircase. Here is a room worthy of a visit from the fact that when the doors are closed the entire apartment is a picture, the whole surface from floor to ceiling, doors included, presenting one painting. The subject is "The Rape of the Sabines."

Now we proceed to the grand drawing-rooms (we have left the state apartments now). Here are several notable acquisitions of art. Among pictures is Sir Joshua Reynolds' portrait of "The Beautiful Duchess" of Devonshire. There is a powerful head of a Jewish Rabbi by Rembrandt, and Titian gives a full-length portrait of Philip II. There are fine portraits, too, of the Archbishop of Spalatro, and of the Admiral Nicola Capella, in Tintoretto's best manner. Holbein gives us a striking full-length of bluff King Hall; and here is a life-size portrait from life of Mary, Queen of Scots, by Zucchero, certainly one of the most pleasing of the presentments that

have come down to us of the pathetic Scottish princess.
There is, further, an expressive portrait of Charles
I.—as a young man—by Cornelius Jansen; while
Dobson gives us the Duke of Albemarle. There are
several striking family portraits, one by Vandyke,
another by Kneller. Observe, likewise, the unfinished
picture by Sir Joshua of Georgina, Countess Spencer,
and her daughter Georgina, afterwards the Duchess
of Devonshire. The noble lady is almost a finished
portrait, but the child's face is amusingly inchoate.
At the end of the room is the Hebe of Canova.
It is a poet's dream of beauty and grace. The spot-
less daughter of Jupiter and Juno is descending from
the skies, and lightly touches with one foot the
throne of Love. In her left hand she holds a cup;
in the right is a pitcher from which she is pouring
out a libation of nectar for a festival of the gods.
In purity of conception and skill in execution this is
a masterpiece of chiselled loveliness. The attitude
is at once easy and animated, and has all the " soft
Paganism " of the Italian master while not lacking
in nerve and force.

"*Here stands the statue that enchants the world*,"
wrote the Poet Rogers of the *Venus de Medici*. The
Chatsworth Hebe runs the Florentine statue very
closely in the contest of surpassing beauty. Chats-
worth is rich in classic chimney-pieces, but the two

in the dining-room are particularly notable. Both are of large dimensions, and executed in the purest Carrara marble. One is the work of Westmacott the younger, and is embellished with life-size figures of Bacchus and Bacchante. Sievier contributes the other, and in this Bacchus is crowned with vine-leaves, and an attendant priestess is replenishing his wine-cup. A Hopton marble plinth, of beautiful colour and lustre, surrounds this apartment; the doorways are of African marble and Siberian jasper. Family portraits adorn the walls. Now, if you please, the picture gallery, the library, and the sculpture gallery await our attention.

We will first visit the Gallery of Paintings, the ceiling of which is painted boldly and well by Sir James Thornhill, who regarded art by the acre, and was the master of one, William Hogarth, a pupil who showed his gratitude to his Gamaliel by running away with his daughter, Mistress Jane. It is not a wild supposition to conjecture that Hogarth himself had something to do with the "historico-allegorico-mural decorations" of Chatsworth while he was serving his apprenticeship under the King's Sergeant-Painter and M.P. The present apartment occupies two sides of the quadrangle, and a profitable hour may be devoted by the earnest art student to its canvases. Here is the original of a picture, with which engravings have made you all familiar, and you approach it as an old friend. It is Sir Edwin Landseer's "Bolton Abbey In the Olden Time." This elaborate composition is certainly one of the most ambitious and most successful of Landseer's efforts. In it you will observe all that charming delineation of animal life which was the painter's distinguishing *metier*. It is shown in the present for the Abbot's table: the dead buck, the fish and fowl, and in the eager dogs held in leash. But combined with this there is an expression of human character in which Landseer surpasses himself. This is seen in the portly Abbot, standing with the quaint breviary under his arm, as he peruses the letter accompanying the gift for the Abbey larder. A study, this portly prelate. He evidently evinces his great gratitude to his Creator by the hearty zest with which he enjoys His gifts; for while monastic culture and strong qualities are displayed in the broad expressive forehead, the luxurious mouth and the Falstaffian corpulency, betray the *gourmand*. Landseer's Abbot is the ideal of the Friar of Orders Grey.

> "*And why I'm so plump the reason I'll tell,*
> *Who lives a good life is sure to live well,*
> *What Baron or Squire, or Knight of the Shire*
> *Lives half so well as a Holy Friar?*
>
> *After supper of heav'n I dream*
> *But that is fat pullets and clouted cream;*

Myself by denial I mortify
With a dainty bit of a warden pie.

I'm cloth'd with sackcloth for my sin,
With old sack-wine I'm lined within,
A chirping cup is my matin song,
And the vesper bell is my bowl, ding dong."

This Abbot is the central figure, but not less studies are the accessories: the attendant Monk, who bears a salver with a wine-glass and flask to refresh the sturdy gamekeeper in charge of the dogs, and the peasant girl offering a basket of speckled trout no doubt fresh from the Wharfe, " the swift Werfe " of Spenser. Unfortunately this modern picture shows signs of deterioration, which are painfully evident in another of Sir Edwin's masterpieces in the same collection: " Laying Down the Law." The colouring in this famous conclave of dogs, this canine *Vehmgericht*, painted within years so recent, is sadly cracking and tesselating, leaving black disfigurements underneath. This premature decay is attributed to defective pigments. Close by this picture you will notice a " Jesus," by Murillo, the tints of which are as pure and as fresh as if laid on but the-day-before-yesterday. Yes, Sir, you are quite right. The old masters painted for posterity, and their colours stand and defy time. Their colour-grinders must have been artists. In a few years, unless the progress of decay is at once arrested, the Chatsworth masterpieces of Landseer will be dear at the price of the frames in which they are hung. Age adds value to the picture of the old master. The worth of the work of the modern painter deteriorates with time. Turner's pictures at the National Gallery are a melancholy example of the reckless adulterating spirit of the age invading Art, and making the painter's colours fleeting frauds. Mr. Holman Hunt is, I am glad to know, interesting himself largely in this question of purity in pigments. It is of vital importance. The posthumous fame of the modern artist is bound up in its issues.

Here you will notice the original of Collins' pleasing picture "Rustic Civility," which a thousand and one engravings and woodcuts have made familiar to us. Here is the "Spartan Isidas," by Eastlake, and represents the youthful Grecian with sword and spear engaging the Theban warriors. It is a very spirited picture. Pass we "The Temptation of St. Anthony," by Tenniers; and a number of family likenesses by Sir Joshua Reynolds, Sir Thomas Lawrence, and other notable portrait painters, to pause before what is, I take it, who, being only "a Guide," and no "art critic," and unable to talk glibly of the corregiosity of Corregio, the most striking picture in the gallery. Here it hangs, and the title is "Monks at Prayer." This surely is one of those examples of art which Mr. Ruskin would say teaches us "what is meant by "painting, as distinguished from plastering, from "rough-casting, from cromo-tinting, from tray-"varnishing, from paper-staining, and from the "sort of things that people in general do when you "put a brush in their hands and a pot within reach "of them." Observe, if you please, the wonderful lighting of the chapel from the upper window at its extremity. The sombre monkish figures are executed in high relief. Every expression of reverence and attitude of devotion is presented. What humility is shown in that bowed head; what intensity of earnest aspiration in those clasped hands, and what pleading fervour of face; what utter self-abnegation in that prostrate figure! The depth of the dark shadows, and the sharp light piercing the window, and the mellower reflection of the tapers, would suggest that the picture is the subtle inspiration of the joint geniuses of Rembrandt and Schkalken. But the painter was Tranet, and the painting formerly belonged to the collection of the Duchess de Berrie. There are other good pictures in this gallery, but I do not wish to give you an "Academy Headache," so hie we to the Library, the pride of the Palace of the Peak.

The perfume of Russian binding, sweetest of odours to Charles Lamb, greets us. The room itself in its structural arrangements and decorations is unique. The circular paintings on the ceiling are the work of a Frenchman of genius, Louis Charon. This Library enshrines, perhaps, the most perfect private collection in the country. Here are books and MSS. so rich and rare that it is impossible to reduce their value to money. The growth of this grand collection has been gradual. Mr. Alfred Wallis, in his appreciative essay on the "Chatsworth Library: Its Founders and Maintainers," remarks:

"This store-house of books was not put together
"like one of the palaces of the Thousand-and-one-
"Nights. It has been formed by the taste and
"learning of several successive generations of the
"Cavendish family from its very start, for some of
"the books are known to have belonged to Sir
"William Cavendish, second husband of the famous
"'Bess of Hardwick,' who sold his own estates in
"the South of England in order to purchase lands
"(Chatsworth amongst the rest) in Derbyshire,
"where his wife had inherited vast territorial pos-
"sessions, and where her own friends and kindred
"lived. A copy of Vitruvius' *De Architectura, libri*
"*X.*, 4to, Argent., 1550, bears his autograph dated
"1557, the year of his death; and we may suppose
"that the work was consulted by him in designing
"the new house which he founded upon the site of

"the old hall of the Leches, from whom Chatsworth
"was purchased, and which remained to be finished
"at his decease. Other books there are in the Library
"which, judging from their date, together with their
"old and worn bindings and the initials, 'W.C.,'
"impressed upon their sides, most probably also
"belonged to him."

These four large volumes are the catalogue of the Library. They are the composition of Sir James Lacaita, and the work is one of the most sumptuous of modern contributions to bibliography. A fifth volume — in course of preparation — will be devoted to the Duke of Devonshire's dramatic rarities. The initial letter of each division of this *magnum opus* is, you will perceive, embellished by a choice quartering from the Cavendish arms. The vignettes adorning the head of each section illustrate the scenery of Chatsworth. In addition to thus tabulating his literary treasures for the benefit of bibliographers, His Grace has cheerfully assented to MM. Braun & Co., of Paris and Dornach, reproducing in permanent autotype about two hundred of the drawings by the old masters which we saw in the Sketch Gallery; while Mr. Richard Keene, of the Art Repository at Derby, has photographed with much success the pictures, the statuary, and rooms of Chatsworth. Books, books, books; to the right of us, to the left of us, in front of us, behind us. In a library of 25,000 volumes even the principal works are too many to enumerate or even to epitomise. Among the MSS. is the Anglo-Saxon MS. of Caedmon, a Benedictionale, executed for Æthelwold, Bishop of Winchester, from 970 to 984. It is a small folio book of 118 leaves of vellum, and Mr. Llewellyn Jewitt, the trustworthy Derbyshire antiquarian, speaks of it as being the most important and finest MS. of the Anglo-Saxon period. The pictures, beautifully coloured, are numerous; the borders are illuminated; and gold and silver are introduced in the illuminations, much in the Byzantine manner. There are other valuable relics of illuminated monastic caligraphy. There is the oldest Florentine edition of Homer, printed on vellum. There is the Mazarine Bible, the first book ever printed. There are the first quartos of dear Will. Shakespeare, and rare impressions of the first productions of Caxton, Wynkyn de Worde, Pynson, and other pioneers of the printing press. But to the artist the most interesting volume is, you will think, the famous *Liber Veritatis* of Claude Lorraine. The extravagant sum of £20,000 was once bid for this unique production. It contains the famous Frenchman's memorandum drawings and sketches of all the pictures that left his easel, and was never intended for the public eye. At his death he left it entailed to his nephews and nieces. Cardinal D'Estrees tried in vain to purchase it for Louis XIV.; but the House of Cavendish secured the "Koh-i-noor of Art" at the expiration of the entail. There is only one other book in the world to compare with it, and that is the wonderful *Liber Studiorum* of Turner's, intended as a rival companion to Claude's volume. It is, perhaps, even more valuable. The colours on Claude's canvasses seem immortal in their soft smoothness; but Turner's pictures are perishing with pathetic completeness, so adulterated were his pigments; and before many years have passed we shall have to turn to the pages of his beautiful *Liber Studiorum* as the only abiding memorial of the painter's poetic genius.

The next room is the Ante-Library. The ceiling is enriched with the paintings of Hayter and Charles Landseer. This compartment in turn gives access to the Cabinet Library, smaller than its companion rooms, but, perhaps, you will regard it as the more beautiful. It has, you see, an ornamented, domed ceiling, divided into decorated apartments, and supported by columns of alabaster and marble, surmounted by Corinthian capitals heavy with gold. The doors are painted to resemble the adjoining bookcases. When closed, all the walls in consequence present an apparently unbroken continuity of books. The sham titles of the "dummy" volumes are the droll conceits of Thomas Hood the Elder. The comic spirit of Momus sports among philosophical tomes, grave histories, and scientific treatises; tickling theologians under the ribs, and behaving with positive levity before solemn jurists and sententious statesmen. Examine the titles of Hood's merry mock library. How should you like to read "Lamb on the Death of Wolfe"? Are your tastes scientific? Here is "Boyle on Steam." Are you an epicure? Here is "Cooke's Specimens of the Sandwich Tongue." What do you think of "Recollections of Bannister by Lord Stair"? Imagine the contents of "Cursory Remarks on Swearing;" and how entertaining must be "Barrow on the Common Weal," "Inigo on Secret Entrances," "Chronological Account of the Date Tree," and "John Knox on Death's Door"! Among other odd titles you have a choice of such *bizarre* books as the following:—"On Cutting off Heirs with a Shilling, by Barber Beaumont;" "Percy Vere, in forty volumes;" "Tadpoles, or Tales out of my own Head;" "Malthus' Attack of Infantry;" "The Life of Zimmermann, by Himself;" "Pygmalion, by Lord Bacon;" "Dirge on the Death of Wolfe, by Lamb;" "Haughtycultural Remarks on London

Pride;" "Voltaire, Volney, Volta, three volumes;" "Campaigns of the British Army, by one of the German Leg.;" "Horn Took on Catching Cows;" "Wren's Voyage to the Canaries;" "Dyspepsia and Heartburn, by the Bishop of Sodor;" "Dibdin's Cream of Tar;" "Minto's Coins;" "Merry's Gay;" "Plane Dealings;" "Ray's Light of Reason;" "Egg, by Shelley;" "Skye, by Mc.Cloud;" "Beveridge on the Beer Act;" "D. Cline on Consumption." This library is in itself a picture; but there are other pictures the design of a greater artist framed by the gilded windows of the palace, in which the entranced eye wanders over light terrace and graceful lawn, sculptured columns and sunlit fountains, to rest on the green undulations of the glorious Park, and the dreamy reaches of the river radiant among the trees, and to the great burly heights, softened with wood, that rise close up all round, like an investing line, to jealously protect the enchanting place from the indignity of the beseiger. Nearly every window at Chatsworth affords a picturesque prospect; and it is a relief sometimes to turn from the overwhelming profusion of splendour within to the repose of the fair landscape without.

And now may I ask your company to the Sculpture Gallery, which, if your stock of admiration is not quite exhausted by the repeated demands already made upon it, will call forth your wonder and praise. A fine gallery more than 100 feet in length and 30 feet in width, lit from the roof, and approached from either the Dining Room or the Orangery. Walls of finely-dressed sandstone; doorcases of marble; entablatures supported by Corinthian columns and pilasters of marble with capitals of gold. We are greeted by the marble figures of two heathen deities which Lord Clare sent from Guzerat. There is a statue of Buddha not artistically noteworthy, but remarkable for the exceeding beauty of the material, which is an almost white nephrite, the Jade of the East. At the other end of this Gallery are two colossal lions in Carrara marble. One is the work of Rinaldi, the other is by Benaglia. Both are copied from Canova's monument to Clement the Fourteenth in St. Peter's at Rome. When I mention that the contributors to the sculptures at Chatsworth include Canova, Thorwaldsen, Schadow, Finelli, Trentanove, Kessels, Tadolini, Albacini, Pozzi, Tenerani, Gibson. Wyatt, Gott, R. Westmacott, Bartolini, Barruzzi, Prosalendi, T. Campbell, Rinaldi, Rennie, Wickmann, Nollekens, Bonelli, and Dantan Jeune, you will admit that the collection is thoroughly representative of both the Continental and English schools, and demands careful inspection and study, and especially so in these days when the significant decadence of the noble art is attracting so much attention and regret in art circles.

It would be difficult to say which of Canova's pieces commands most approval: his Endymion sleeping, with his dog watching at his feet, or his statue of the mother of the first Napoleon. The classic shepherd is a very poetical conception, poetically executed, and on the marble face of the young sleeper is that magic beauty that drew Diana to the slopes of Mount Latmos to gaze on its loveliness. The *Mater Napoleonis*, on the other hand, is a masterpiece of pose and expression. The historic Corsican lady is represented in a position half-sitting, half-reclining, an attitude of meditative composure. One arm rests upon the back of an antique chair, and the figure is clothed with drapery that is a study in the natural grace of its lines. The face is beautiful, but intellectual strength and commanding dignity are the leading characteristics of the features. It is a sad, pensive face, that bears no resemblance whatever to that of her son, the Warrior-Emperor, which is close by, a colossal bust also by Canova. This characteristic likeness has also much of the ideal character of ancient Greek sculpture, and invites comparison with Antonio Canova's other conception of "The Little Corporal," the undraped one in the possession of the Duke of Wellington at Apsley House. Napoleon naked, and yet noble in his nudeness! Such was Canova's power; and it was of this classic craftsman that an empty English aristocrat asked upon his decease "who is going to carry on his business?" Who, indeed?*

The same chisel gives us likewise a bust of the late Duke of Devonshire, and a bust of Petrarch's Laura. Now behold "The Filatrice, or Spinning Girl," by Schadow—a young girl diverting herself with a ball of thread and a spindle. Ideal beauty and natural ease are combined in the figure with great success. This

---

* In this connection "G. A. S.," whose critical knowledge of graphics and plastics is greater than that of any of his contemporaries, writes: "I may ask fairly, without fear of contradiction, whether, with the exception of Napoleon, there is a single historical personage of modern times whose form could be practically presented undraped? What should we say to a naked Brougham, a naked William Pitt—imagine their noses!—an undraped Peel, a disrobed Gladstone, a Beaconsfield 'mid nodings on'? Napoleon I. in Canova's statue bears, with triumphant success, the crucial test of the nude. You forget that he is a little man—not only little, but actually 'stumpy'—you forget all the spiteful libels of Michelet about his having had no eyebrows, and his hair being normally of a sandy-brown, but darkened by pomatum. You see only the classic hero, as classic as the Antinous, as classic as the Apollo Belvedere, as classic as the Discobolos, and heroic enough to hold, as Canova's statue holds the effigy of Victory in his conquering right hand."

CHATSWORTH.

Venus is Thorwaldsen's; that Wyatt's. Passing on we come to Gibson's "Mars and Cupid." Here is the "Cymbal Player" by Westmacott, the "Wounded Achilles" is by Albicini, and the "Cupid and Psyche" by Finelli. Full of artistic grace is the group by Tanerani: "Cupid Extracting a Thorn from the Foot of Venus;" and I would particularly invite your attention to the bas-reliefs of surpassing excellence by Thorwaldsen, the severe sculptor of the north, representing "Night" and "Morning;" then we will proceed to the Orangery where sculptured marble shines white among the dark and light greens of the plants.

We have now seen all that portion of the House which is thrown open to the public. Other apartments, not less beautiful, are occupied by the Duke of Devonshire's and the Marquis of Hartington's private suites of rooms. These are rich in art glories, and include, among many other treasures, a series of landscapes and sea-pieces by Carmichael, and a wonderfully sculptured fountain-piece representing "Venus at the Bath." But with these rooms we have nothing to do. Still our tour of inspection is not completed. If Chatsworth is delightful indoors, it is none the less charming out-of-doors, with its terraces and lawns, its French Garden: a forest of tall columns crowned with busts and trellised with leaves; its fountains and cascades, and its great conservatory, from which the idea of the Crystal Palace was taken. A visit to Chatsworth would be woefully incomplete without a glance at these, and lo! here is Mr. T. Speed himself, who succeeded Sir Joseph Paxton, as Gardener in Chief, and he will take us from the bleak moors of the Peak into sun-fed palm lands, and we shall wander in a glass-closed world among flowers and fruits and fountains, sweet smells and pleasing colours.

HADDON HALL:

AN AUTUMNAL VIGNETTE.

"The light still shines through the latticed pane
  As it shone to them, and the shadowed door
Is the shadow they saw, and the stains remain
  Of the wine they spill'd on the daïs floor.
The river that runs by the old Hall's walls
  Murmured to them as it murmurs now;
The golden glow of the sunlight falls,
  As it fell for them, on glade, river, and bough;
The hall where they feasted, the church where they
    prayed,
  Their cradles, and chambers, and gravestones, stay;
While lord and vassal, youth and maid,
  Knight and lady, have passed away."

The Peak district is rich in historic piles. If it be true that Mr. Ruskin said he could not get along in a country where there were no castles, Derbyshire should be his delight. There is William Peveril's crumbling fortress at Castleton; the old abbey ruin at Deepdale; while Hardwicke Hall, Bolsover Castle, and Wingfield Manor may be said to be neighbours.

But Haddon Hall stands pre-eminent among these histories in stone, an ancient anthem in architecture. Behold its grey battlements and turrets and towers, half-smothered in fading foliage, looking over the windings of the Wye. It is an October afternoon, and the autumn-time is, perhaps, the best of all periods of the year to see Haddon Hall. The colour of the woods is now in harmony with the pensive grey stone of the baronial battlements. The foliage, no longer an uniform, monotonous green, is a study of intense tints. The tresses of the lady-birch are spangled with yellow. Bronzes and russets and coppery reds are mixed up with the dark green of the solemn yews. The beech-trees gleam with rose-colour. The brilliant beads of the mountain ash burn amid the soft brown of ripening nuts and the sober hues of wild berries. The woods are silent. A solitary robin's note on the terrace intensifies the stillness. Faded leaves fall at our feet with a musical sigh. The river is running away with argosies of yellow leaves. The autumnal sadness suits the deserted old towers of Haddon. The castle itself is almost as perfect now as in the feudal days of chivalry, when its walls echoed the noisy revelry of retainers, and the wassail-cup went its merry round. The place seems as if Sir George Vernon, "the King of the Peake," and his retinue had just left it for a day's hunting in the woods, and would be back again anon. The marks of their whittles, and the stains of their trenchers, are on the massive tables in the old banqueting hall. One of the huntsmen has left his horn behind him in yonder little room. The modern tourist could no more sound it than bend Ulysses' bow. There are also a gigantic pair of jack-boots, and a thick leathern doublet, should you wish to follow Sir George's party into the forest. That fireplace in the kitchen, with its incalculable capacity for fuel, is ready to deal summarily with a fat stirk; but coals are now, alas! twenty shillings a ton, and steaks are at famine price. In the state bed-room, where Queen Elizabeth slept, the bed seems to have just been made. The old ball-room, with its oaken floor and big window recesses, is deserted; but it does not need a wild imagination to people it with the guests of the past. I can hear the echo of the bygone revelry. The minstrel is tuning his harp in praise of a "ladye faire." Young squires and country belles are dancing, who have been dust these two hundred years. The sun shines on the silent terrace, where the mind's eye sees a peacock spreading the rainbow glories of its tail, and beholds a garden party that might have lent inspiration to Watteau. In the quadrangle yonder, to which that vassal in buff jerkin is hurrying, is a hunting group that Wouvermanns might have immortalised. Dorothy Vernon has just stolen past to have a whispered interview with John Manners. Here is the spreading elm, under whose leafy gloom he used to wait at night for a hushed word of love, or a warning wave of the hand, from the little oriel window in the tower above. He is cutting her initials on the bark, just as Rosalind's name was carved on the trees by a man who haunted the forest. A pretty "bit" for an artist is Dorothy Vernon's doorway, from whence she eloped:

"*Into the night, and the arms of love.*"

A painter has placed his easel in front of it, and the heavy old oaken door, and eleven worn stone steps, are having their picturesque sadness thrown upon the canvas. Haddon Hall is indeed haunted by painters. I never pay it a visit but some artists are breathing the ancient air of the place. To-day, a lady of the easel has found a fascinating study in the old tapestry of "My Lady's Chamber;" another artist is sketching an old doorway, with quaint stone carvings, and bleached timber, studded with nails red with rust. A third painter is in love with the avenue of lime-trees forming the upper terrace, and known as "Dorothy Vernon's Walk." Haddon Hall does not depend upon a love legend for its fame, but the story of Dorothy Vernon gives it a human interest that still more endears the baronial mansion to the followers of the picturesque. We are told that there is no foundation for the tender tradition; and even so respectable an antiquarian as Mr. John Charles Cox is of opinion that Dorothy "never eloped at all, but was married after the usual humdrum fashion." This is the age of unbelief. Robin Hood is regarded as a myth; Shakespeare is voted an impostor; even the Bible is reduced by scientists and sceptics into a piece of Hebrew mythology; and, of course, the sweet old romance of Haddon Hall must be duly dispelled, Mr. Gradgrind, by "facts, sir, facts." But, nevertheless, the Goths and Vandals will not quite destroy the old romance. It is one of the poems we must not willingly let die. Three hundred chequered years have passed, but still the legend is charming and new; and many budding springs shall bloom into summer, and the summers soften into autumn, and the autumns wither into winters wild and cold, before we discredit the sweet story of John Manners donning the woodman's garb, and sleeping with the hinds of the forest, in order that he might be near his Dorothy; of the midnight elopement from the brilliant ballroom; of the runaway ride through the black night, and of the marriage in Leicester Forest, where

P

Dorothy's heart promised far more than was demanded by the Prayer Book.

It is a walk for poet and painter by the Wye side from Haddon either to Rowsley or Bakewell. There are pictures all the way—suggestive studies of old gnarled trees hanging over the voiceful water, ideal vistas of meadow with wooded heights beyond, "bits" of the old-world mixed up with trees and torrent. At Bakewell, if the Haddon Hall romance is still strong within you, there is the fine old church, with the Vernon monuments. There rest in their long sleep Sir George Vernon, and his two wives, the Dames Margaret and Maud. Beside them are "Sir John Manners, of Haddon, Knight," and "Dame Dorothie, his wife." The runaway daughter awaits the Resurrection morning at her father's side; and the austere step-mother and the proscribed lover are reconciled in death.

HUNTING IN THE HIGH PEAK.

"There are soul-stirring chords in the fiddle and flute
　When dancing begins in the hall,
And a goddess in muslin, that's likely to suit,
　Is mate of your choice for the ball;
But the player may strain every finger in vain,
　And the fidler may rosin his bow,
Nor flourish nor string such a rapture shall bring,
　As the music of sweet Tally-ho!

There's a melody, too, in the whispering trees
　When day has gone down in the West,
And a lullaby soft in the sigh of the breeze
　That hushes the woods to their rest:
There are madrigals fair in the voices of air,
　In the stream with its ripple and flow,
But a merrier tune shall delight us at noon,
　In the music of sweet Tally-ho!"

WHYTE-MELVILLE.

"I think the girls have gone mad," was the Old Lady's remark as **every room** at Limecliffe Firs seemed to resound with silvery shouts of "Hark forrard!" "Tally-ho!" "Yoicks!" "Hey, ho, chevy!" and other exclamations, ecstatic but inexplicable, peculiar to the vocabulary of huntsmen.

It was a December evening preceding a meet of the Buxton and Peak Forest Harriers. The Young Man was to join the hunt. It had also been arranged that the two young ladies and the present writer should drive to the scene of action in the pony carriage.

This had not been settled without some protest from the prudent Old Lady. She remembers the gloom of a certain grey November day in the years agone when the dangers of the chase were personally illustrated at Limecliffe Firs. But a broken limb has not diminished the Young Man's ardour. It was amusing to hear the animated logic with which he overcame the opposition of the solicitous Mother of the Gracchi. His arguments were founded on both moral and physical grounds.

"A run with the harriers"—he contended—"promotes health, fosters courage, requires judgment, teaches perseverance, developes energy, tries patience, tests temper, and exercises every true virtue. It is recreation to the mind, joy to the spirits, strength to the body. To be a good huntsman was to be a fine manly fellow: a 'muscular Christian,' if you like, but a 'muscular Christian' as was Charles Kingsley, the patentee of the phrase. Fishing teaches patience; but just look, my nephew, at the number of moral lessons inculcated by hunting. Care and diligence are required 'to find.' 'Look before you leap' was an aphorism of practical wisdom derived from Nimrod and not Solomon; while 'Try Back' was another phrase which might be wisely applied to daily life. 'Try Back' when an obstinate hound misleads a pack, and it is found that the trail so diligently sought is hopelessly lost. 'Try Back' renews hope and rewards perseverance. 'Try Back,' then, in the larger field of life, with its vexations, disappointments, lost chances, and broken hopes. If led into error, 'Try Back;' if success is denied thee in that wearisome up-hill toil, 'Try Back;' baffled, blighted, broken-on-the-wheel, 'Try Back.' Is thy trust betrayed, and thy love false? Then 'Try Back.' There is a false scent somewhere; a mistake has been made at some critical juncture, so 'Try Back,' and a second quest shall give thee splendid recompense."

There was much more of this eloquent hunting homily, which threw such a glamour of sentiment over hares and horses and harriers that the Old Lady, fond of sermons, gradually relented in her scruples. She finally surrendered when she heard that hunting the hare took precedence of fox hunting, since the fox did not afford half so much genuine sport, and while the flesh of the former was delicious, that of the latter was so much filthy vermin.

I cannot go the length of giving the hunting of the High Peak a place before that of the Quorn Country; but the wild picturesqueness of North Derbyshire, with its loose stone walls and steep mountain declivities, imparts a charm and an excitement to the sport which is unknown to the red-coated horsemen of the monotonously flat fields of Leicestershire. The wonder is that Buxton in the winter season does not become as much a hunting centre as Melton Mowbray or Market Harbro'. There are three packs of harriers of established reputation, meeting twice or thrice a week within easy distance of the popular watering place. These are the Dove Valley Harriers that answer the wild "Tally-Ho!" in the picturesque landscape watered by the Dove; the High Peak Harriers that have their meets either at Parsley Hay, a Wharf on the High Peak line of railway, Newhaven, a solitary hostelry at the meeting of several roads, and a famous house enough in the coaching days, or at Over Haddon, by the Lathkill Dale; and the Buxton and Peak Forest Harriers, which generally start from Peak Forest, or from Dove Holes, and pursue the rough and romantic country side historically famous as the hunting ground of kings.

It was the latter pack that the Young Man had elected to follow on the morning after that December evening when the house was **alive** with silvery echoes of **the** hunting **field. The weather had** during the past week **or two** attested **that there was** something radically wrong with the **Zodiac ; but on** that night, **as** we looked out **from the glow and** warmth **of the** room, the **air was keen and** clear; the **moon** shone with an intense **white electric** light; **the roofs** glittered in **the cold radiance ;** every detail of architecture **was revealed in a sharp relief** that made the shadows ebony **in their deepness; the gas** lamps burned with **a** dirty yellow ; **but there was not** enough frost to affect the morrow's enjoyment.

A grey morning **follows that** glistening **night.** The mist lies thick upon the **hills. The meet is at** Dove Holes **at twelve ;** and the Young Man, with the snow **of** sixty winters **in** his beard, seems part **of his** chesnut cob as **he** rides in black coat, green **vest, and** corduroys, by the side **of** our pony carrriage. Raw and cold is the dull ride across Fairfield Common; but we have **foot** warmers in **the** conveyance, and quite a panoply of soft shawls ; while it makes one feel quite snug and warm to contemplate the sealskin of Somebody and the furs of Sweetbriar. Who is it who writes :—

> *"The sleekest otter cuffs—*
>   *The **rosiest** of real skin—*
> *The **sable-est** of muffs—*
>   *The softest gloves of sealskin.*

> *The quaintest hose with clocks,*
> *A cloud like a mantilla*
> *The velvetest of frocks—*
> *Wears little sweet Chinchilla."*

Presently the sun warms the grey fog until the country seems to float in a golden mist; a mellow amber light, such as Turner and Claude Lorraine loved to introduce in a poetic atmospheric effect. There is animation at Dove Holes. A score or more well-mounted horsemen make picturesque patches against the ridges of sombre hills; there are one or two farmers on well ribbed-up horses; there is a lady, well-known to the county as a bold rider, on a sturdy grey mare that is pawing with impatience to charge the stone walls; there is an old gentleman with the gout in a bath-chair, who is anxious to witness the "throw off;" there are one or two carriages and antiquated gigs; while the number of camp-followers on foot show how potent is the spell of sport among all classes when "the Horn of the Hunter is heard on the Hill." The keen harriers are with the huntsman, Joe Etchells, the men and boys on foot are grouped around, and take an intelligent interest in the preliminary proceedings. There is the Judge Thurlow look of wisdom on canine countenances, solemn in its sagacity. Presently the Master is seen riding along the road from Buxton, with other well-known members of the Buxton and

Peak Forest Hunt. Somebody, who regards everything from what Thackeray called "**a paint pot spirit**," talks of the hunting groups of Wouvermann, and the horses and hounds of Rosa Bonheur. Sweetbriar is intently silent: but she makes, nevertheless, a very pretty element in the picture.

And now, behold! the first quest is successful, and cavalry and infantry are instantly scattered in picturesque disorder. It is a picture full of movement; and the broken undulating features of the country, with broad **valleys and** bold hills, show it up in all its artistic charm. The present hare, however, soon succumbs, and the hounds are thereby "encouraged." And now the wiry Master **of the Pack** gives the order for a second quest. **The cry** comes that another hare has "gone away!" She is in full flight; the alert hounds follow in swift pursuit; this time the chase grows exciting. People who derive their notion of Puss from Cowper's hares have an attractive lesson **in** natural history prepared for them by a hunt with the harriers. The celerity of the mountain hare is only exceeded by its subtlety, which exceeds even the cunning of Master Reynard. The intellect of the hunter and the instinct of the hounds are taxed to the uttermost by the shifts and doubles and dodges of their "quarry." The buck hare, now, after making a turn or two about his "form," will frequently lead the hunt five or six miles before he will turn his head. But madam is more wily. **She delights in** harrassing and embarrassing the hounds. **She** seldom makes out end-ways before her pursuers, but trusts to sagacity rather than speed. See! now she is off and the harriers are in hot pursuit. Riders are spurring their horses up the slope. A good **run** at **last**, we say. The **harriers** are well-nigh their prey. Puss sees the intervening distance lessening; **for a** hare, mark you, like a rabbit, looks behind; and suddenly she throws herself with a jump **in a** lateral direction and lies motionless. The manœuvre is a success. The hounds fly past deceived by the diplomatic twist. They pull up at last exasperated. The scent is lost.

"These 'ill 'ares is as fawse as Christians," says a beefy-faced country **man, with** steaming breath. Pedestrians appear to have an advantage over the horsemen. Only at intervals comes the **wild and** thrilling cross-country "charge of the light brigade," the spurred galop that belongs to stag or fox-hunting. The rest is made up of occasional spurts and pauses, for the hare's flight is made in circles. The infantry can thus keep the cavalry in constant sight. Sometimes, indeed, they have better chances than the mounted Nimrods.

Another "find." The harriers are now "getting down" to the deceptive turnings of Puss. The wild rush clearly won't do, they intuitively argue; and so with strange intelligence they resolve to keep themselves in head, and, with nose to ground, determine to checkmate the craft of the game with a responsive **craft.** They take the trail up with intellectual **sagacity.** Finding her "doublings" of little use now, Puss makes across a turnip field for the hill. "She's for Peak Forest or Sparrow Pit!" is the cry of the crowd. The pack plod up hill. "Hark to Watchman!" "Follow Watchman!" is the hurried command. The lady of the hunt is now neatly leading. Esau follows. The young man is showing his sturdy back to a field of flagging horses. A narrow stream, tumbling between steep banks over rocky boulders, presents itself. Some of the horsemen seek an easier avenue. One, more adventurous, who rides in a long mackintosh coat, takes a "header" in the water. He scrambles out soaked to the skin. "A good job tha' browt thi' macintosh wi' thee!" says a consoling country friend to the dripping rider as he seeks the bank of the stream.

It is "bellows to mend" before the steep stony summit of Beelow is reached. We can see the white steam from the horses' nostrils. The hare, being able to run faster up hill than down, has the pull over horse and hound. Before the top of the stubborn hill is gained, however, she has a premonition of danger ahead. A sudden turn; and she bounds through a flock of sheep and under the very legs of the horses toiling up the ungrateful ascent. The hounds turn and tear down after the scent in relentless pursuit. A stout farmer comes a crucial cropper over a stone wall. Half of the loose limestone boulders fall over him. "Oh! is he hurt?" demands Somebody with startled solicitude, while horse and rider lie together. "Noa, not 'im; he's non hurt; ha fell on 'is yed," says a sympathetic yeoman at the post of our observation.

Now puss takes the wall, and passes down the road. She skirts the very wheels of our carriage. We see her startled brown eyes, the long hair about the quivering mouth, the beautiful silky ears thrown back in an agony of strained alertness; the soft colour of her winter fur. Fly past the dogs. Come the hunters. Boys on foot beat galloping horses in their fleetness. There is a wild clamour as the pack pelter down hill. It is irresistible. The excitement is intoxicating. Somebody and Sweetbriar are racing after the pursuers. Even the gouty old gentleman in the bath-chair gets out and hobbles along as if he had lost his head. A woman from a cottage close by rushes out with a frying pan in her hand; while among the crowd is a village bootmaker, with his hat off and his apron on. I have known staid tradesmen on similar occasions also take to flight at the thrill of the clear "Tally-ho!" men, mark you, who are as sedate and phlegmatic as Dutchmen under any other circumstances, and never knew a faster pulse of life.

Lo! the hare doubles again; but the harriers are upon her. We are close by at the finish. Poor Puss utters a death-cry, piercing in its helpless pathos. It is like the sobbing appeal of a child. Sweetbriar begs for the doomed life to be saved; and the exasperated harriers, eager for blood, are driven off, so that she may have the beautifully shaded coat. But the timid creature is dead, and the frightened eyes are glazed.

When the hunters get together in close company, there are one or two black coats, green vests, and corduroys that are dabbed in dirt, and nearly every horse is blowing, after the sharp burst over the hilly country. Refreshment is in demand at a roadside tavern. The beverage most in favour is a curious alcoholic mixture, very popular among Derbyshire huntsmen, and known as "thunder-and-lightning." It is composed of hot old ale, ginger, sugar, nutmeg, and gin. On paper this appears a dreadful draught, worthy of Lucrezia Borgia; but the eagerness with which it is quaffed this December afternoon is practical proof of the inspiring effect of the stirrup-cup on the exhausted Actæons of the Peak.

This is the last run of the day, for the short-lived sun is setting in red behind the moorland edges, and the amber mist is deepening into fog. We drive home in the waning light, exhilarated with the stirring incidents of the day. The young Man has much to tell us, as he ambles along by our side, of spirited passages in the hunt which had escaped us, and which sound like an Iliad to our ears.

At Limecliffe Firs to-night we discuss at supper the plump hare of the hunt, whose pitiful cry of pain we heard as it died. And we find that the healthful air, the joyous freedom, the excitement and the exercise of the day, have made us too grossly gastronomical to feel sentimental over devouring our victim.

But why is Sweetbriar absent from the table?

A CRUISE ROUND CASTLETON.

"Those grim and horrid caves,
  Whose looks affright the day,
Wherein nice Nature saves
  What she would not bewray,
Our better leisure craves
  And doth invite our lay."
                    MICHAEL DRAYTON.

A bit of Blue John spar! I use it as a paper-weight. It must be dismissed from that office. It has such a tendency at times to catch my eye and send me wandering off on the wings of Memory far away from the business concernments to which I should be applying myself with engrossed earnestness. This inanimate thing has a motive power that carries me away up to Peveril's Castle in the Peak, and to "A Cruise on Wheels," Kalmat and I took through the valleys of the Castleton country, and the flight opens out recollections of other pleasant trips I have taken in the same good company. I am thus wafted away from practical pursuits, and am rudely aroused from the rapture of retrospect to discount myself as a very dreamy and ideal individual who wants a lot of romantic rubbish knocking out of his head by Mr. Gradgrind. There was an enchanted carpet in the Arabian Nights' Entertainment which transported you wherever you would be at a wish. The most commonplace things possess this talismanic power to carry you away mentally to other scenes and back to other days. The law of association links things which to the eyes of other people seem trite and trivial with the most glowing memories, recalling pleasures of the past to gild the gloom of the present, and borrowing the sunshine of yesterday to chase away the clouds that have gathered to-day. An alpen-stock, mixed up in a dusty litter of fishing rods, gaff-hooks, and landing nets, is, for instance, an Aaron's rod of magic that summons back all the glow and inspiration of a Swiss holiday, and revives some half-forgotten passages of life in bright and minute detail. The sight of the binding of a neglected copy of *Murray* transports you from worry and trouble and sombre surroundings to the far-off mountain side and remote sea-shore. It seems to carry with it an aroma that is as the ozone of the ocean and the ether of the moorland. The fast fading photograph of a yacht

hanging up in your study acts like necromancy to
take you again amid the lonely islands, the lovely
colours, and the magical sunsets of the Western
Highlands, and has the power to make the weary
Faust of matter-of-fact life fresh and buoyant as the
crested waves that tore past that pleasure craft.
The same law of association imparts the poetry and
pathos of a life to a withered forget-me-not crushed
between a faded letter; and endows a tress of soft
hair, treasured in the sacred recesses of a secret
drawer, with a spell of sentiment that the lapse of
long years only renders stronger. That hidden
baby's glove, bitten at the thumb, and that tiny pair
of blue shoes, start sobs that the mother thought
had long ago been stifled. The sight of an old
letter to the most unemotional of us will restore
with a strange thrill "the touch of a vanished hand,
and the sound of a voice that is still." A photo-
graphic album crowds your lonely room with a jovial
company, and fills it with many a cheery laugh, good
old chorus, and wholesome joke. Tears flood the
eyes of Charles Reade's rough outcasts in the
Australian bush, as they listen to an English lark
pouring out its full soul in an ecstacy of song from
a wicker-cage hung over the door of a settler's log-
hut; for the little feathered minstrel is connected
by no common ties with fond ingle-nooks and quiet

churchyards left behind thousands of leagues of stormy sea. One of Bret Harte's rough miners in the Western land remarks apologetically to his partner "I must write a letter home," as he sees a fresh-faced English girl passing the gulch at a crossing where they are working. The same subtle spirit of association was at work in both instances.

And so it is that this piece of fluor spar touches the chords of Memory, and they respond in a sympathetic song of other days. It calls forth sweet perfumes from the flowery fields of retrospect. It is like the simple sea shell on your mantle-shelf, which, although exiled many miles from its shingly shore, still echoes the murmur of the waves. A bit of Blue John! It is an unfailing index to the volume of recollection: an entertaining book to read, notwithstanding Mr. Alfred Tennyson's philosophy, which is borrowed from Malesherbes, who borrowed it from Dante, that "a Sorrow's Crown of Sorrow is remembering happier things." There is, indeed, no pleasanter pastime than that of visiting the sunny spots of memory when

"*Our yesterdays look backward with a smile,
Nor, like the Parthian, wound us as they fly.*"

But a truce to these digressive didactics. Let Blue John tell his story.

Kalmat, the traveller in many lands, who is at last finding out the neglected beauty spots of his own country, has before been introduced, and is now on speaking terms with you. He is my comrade for a Whitsuntide Trip. Whitsuntide, of the three great English holidays, is surely the most delightful. While Christmas is purely a festival of the fireside and of sentiment; and Easter is a chilling compromise between winter and spring; Whitsuntide has all the green beauty of opening summer. And the Whitsuntide of our wandering is all that the holiday maker could desire. Kalmat had often heard of Castleton and its caves, and the romantic dales frowned upon by Abney and Derwent Edge; and we had months before decided to drive there from Buxton, and from thence back, by pleasant stages and a roundabout route, through the heart of the healthful hilly country. The delights of "A Cruise upon Wheels," are known only to those who have read the breezy book of that name, and to the greater constituency who have been charmed with "The Strange Adventures of a Phæton," although they have found nothing particularly "strange" or "adventurous" in that tempting trip taken by Queen Titania, Bonny Bell, and Count Von Rosen, along the old country highways and sweet-smelling lanes from Middlesex to Mid-Lothian. The word "Cruise" aptly describes our journey. The mountain air is as exhilarating as a sea breeze; and how often does the immensity of moorland meeting the sky suggest the ocean to our fancy? We are, moreover, bound to no beaten track. We can steer into out-of-the-way bays, and call at will at little havens off the direct line of travel. We are not obliged to sail straight on, but can drop our anchor as an idle caprice takes us, and leave the ship (I mean the trap) in charge of the cabin-boy (that is the stable lad), whenever we choose to fish or sketch. We have our fishing rods on board, and carry two guns.

"Give 'er 'er 'ed," is the admonition of Twitty, the barrel-like Boots at Kalmat's Hotel, who might have stepped out of Charles Dickens' pages as a living illustration of Mr. Samuel Weller. A pungent humourist when occasion demands is the familiar functionary. I tell Kalmat some of his stories as we bowl across Fairfield Common in the fresh fluent air and vivid blueness of this June morning. The most Twittyesque relates to a time when he carried the luggage of a celebrated but selfish old lawyer from the Old Hall Hotel to the railway station. The legal luminary had been staying at the hotel for several weeks. During that period Twitty had given unwonted lustre to his boots, and the services of no common valet. At the station the departing visitor "tipped" him with the stupendous sum of—sixpence! Twitty regarded the insignificant silver with a gaze in which astonishment mingled with contempt. Then he said—

"What is this for, sir?"

"For you, my man."

"For me, sir," said the baffled Boots, with exasperated voice and defiant manner, "Do you know what I have done for you, sir?"

"Do not be impertinent! Remember to whom you are speaking," remonstrated the future judge, astonished at Twitty's impudence.

"I do not forget it, sir!" rejoined Boots to the Bar, with a withering scorn that was in itself a lesson in elocution. "I don't forget it, sir. You are a Lawyer—I'm a Boots. You black paper—I black boots. You use a pen—I use a brush. Mine takes a polish—yours don't. *There's not so much d——d difference when you come to hanalyze it!*" and the repudiated sixpence was tossed into the air, and Twitty walked away with offended dignity expressed in face and figure.

Stories of this Wellington de Boots have taken us past Fairfield, when we come to the conclusion that twelve more uninteresting miles could not well be found in Derbyshire than the dozen which serve to separate Buxton from Castleton. But it is something to be out on such a day as this, and our mare seems to know it, and at a merry pace we skirt the old road once traversed by Roman chariots. We bowl along past the lime-kilns at Dove Holes, past the bygone Barmoor Clough toll-gate, and then, leaving the main road, turn at a sharp angle to the right and breast the hill. Close here is the Ebbing and Flowing Well, celebrated by a thousand-and-one guide-book writers—surer of their genius than their grammar, and finer in their fancy than faithful in their facts—as one of the Wonders of the World. But there is nothing now about this pool for the pen to cry out "eloquent in the elegancies of Iambics," as Mr. Ruskin's double put it to the studious youth of classic Chesterfield. Truth, like murder, must out. The famous Ebbing and Flowing Well is in truth a horse-pond which serves as a watering-place for the cattle of the adjoining pastures. This pond is supplied by a spring of intermittent action, from which water flows at intervals. The wetness or dryness of the weather governs the frequency of the action of the well. Sometimes as much as 120 hogsheads of water are reputed to rise and disappear. Rustic ignorance connects the phenomenon with the ebbing and flowing of the tide at Liverpool. Practical science, however, explodes the wonder by illustrating the motion of the spring by that of a common syphon. In the same neighbourhood the same mystery is repeated. "Water-swallows" is the name locally given to these springs. When Mr. Charles Middlewick was at Vesuvius, the fiery mountain was not in a state of eruption, much to the subsequent disappointment of Papa Perkyn Middlewick, who contended that his son ought to have "hinsisted on a ruption. I spared no hexpense, Charley; I didn't stint ye; I told yer to go in for everything." The Derbyshire Ebbing and Flowing Well is not flowing for Kalmat to-day, and I want him to go in for everything. But no matter. The mare responds to the crack of the whip. The sun smiles upon the stony scenery as if to soften its bleak stern character, and to melt with sympathetic warmth its rigid angularities; smiles upon sheep asking for bread and getting stones, for the limestone crops up in boulder growth above the scanty grass; upon treeless fields ruled out in low rising and falling walls of cold grey stone that strike harshly to the eye accustomed to the grateful green hedges of southern pastures, and the lavish luxuriance of southern lanes; upon the hard-faced outline of swelling hill and sweeping valley, in which the sun searches out dainty tones of colour, communicated by lichen and moss, heathbell and bracken. Comes the village of Sparrow Pit. The diverging road leads to Peak Forest, where the chapelry was once extra-parochial and extra-episcopal. This made the village an English Gretna Green. Runaway couples, and politic people desirous of contracting hasty marriages, hastened here from all parts of England. Legend has lent the horror of a romantic murder to one of these clandestine marriages at what was in the "good old days" a lonely hamlet lost among the hills. It is a tale of bur-r-l-lud! Dithery music. Lights low. Dress of the last century. Two runaway lovers, as rich in money as in love, returning from a matrimonial visit to the Peak Forest Parson, who if he brought no soul to salvation, was, no doubt instrumental in bringing a good many couples to a state of repentance. They are on horseback on their happy way Hallamshire-ward. In the gloomy pass of the Winnats are a band of murderers, who waylay them and still their warm hearts for ever, simply for the sake of their personal possessions. Kalmat says English civilization has not improved so much since then, for an old man was murdered the other day in one of the Home Counties for—sixpence. We shall soon be at the scene of the dreadful deed. The place is supposed to be still haunted by the victims of the tragedy. When the winter wind screams down the narrow pass on a wild night, local superstition associates the weird sound with the death cry of the lovers, and shiveringly cowers under the bedclothes.

Here is Perryfoot. What a beautiful green, soon to be dimmed into a dingier hue, has spread over the plantation to the left. The mass of bleak limestone mountain to the right, standing out in rounded outline in the sunny air, is Eldon Hill. Midway up its steep side is Eldon Hole: a chasm once reputed to be fathomless. Poetry has made it one of the Profundities of the Peak in the Latin verse of Hobbes. Science has invested it with awe and mystery in Catcott's "Deluge." Tradition establishes it as a place of blood-curdling horror. Among other terrible tales told of this perpendicular abyss, it is said that in the reign of Queen Elizabeth the Earl of Leicester had a man let down with ropes into the dark cavity. When drawn up he was dumb and died in mad contortions. He had seen—But no matter. "A good joke for the mighty Earl, but rather hard lines for his human plummet," says Kalmat. Some of the guide books have worked themselves up into throes of thrilling excitement over similar traditions; but much of the "thunder" is taken away when it is known that the hole has been thoroughly explored by capable scientists, and that the bottom was found at a depth of 70 yards. So we will not, Kalmat, steer out of our course to inspect the awful abyss.

Polyphemus no longer dwells in this Cave of the Cyclopés, and we have no Achæmenides to let down with the sacrificial rope.

The road winds among the treeless hills, beautiful in their very bleakness. The pasturage of the moorland sheep is enamelled with the gold of the mountain pansy. A lark is the only spot in the bright blueness of the sky. The vertical sun reveals every undulation of the landscape in its strong white light. There is the hum of bees. Young plovers are making trial trips on their newly-fledged wings. All round a hundred pictures of hill and valley, lonely peak and deep hollow, rounded knoll and sweeping ridge; here and there a clump of storm-rent pines; now and again a solitary farmstead. Presently we reach the head of the path leading through the romantic paths of the Winnats. We disembark at these straits, and, sending our craft round to Castleton by the steep Mam Tor road, proceed on foot. There is excellent anchorage at the Bull's Head, and the midshipmite unfurls his flag (that is his whip) and gets under way in good style. "The best and most forcible sense of a word "is often that which is contained in its etymology," says Coleridge; and this mountain pass giving access to Castleton is described in its name: Winnats, or "windgates." The ravine presents a natural passage for the mountain winds that sweep through it and wail and moan and howl and scream; while its particular situation is such as to collect in hollow and angle the breezes from each point of the compass. This rift is one of Nature's romantic openings in the mountain limestone. Narrow is the path between the perilous and precipitous crags. The rocky confinement brings out in beautiful *chiaroscuro* the gleam of grey limestone, the green of clinging verdure, and the gloom of changing shadows. Kalmat—accustomed to some of the wildest passages in Alpine scenery, and familiar with the Sierràs of the Far West—stands enchanted in this grand nook which is an hour's journey only from swarthy Sheffield, and but half-a-day's trip from toiling and moiling Manchester. It is a romance in rock; a petrified poem; a lyric in limestone. The rock-ribbed gorge grows more striking in its revelations of savage sublimity as we pursue the pathway. The rocks tower to greater and wilder heights. They assume castellated shapes. Now there is the crude suggestion of cathedral turret and tower; then threaten fortress and bastion. The carving might be the rough sculpture of the Giants and Gods of mythology. Near the extremity of the pass which is something like a mile in length, a huge sentinel tor disputes further progress. We seem locked in among the lonely limestone precipices, awful in their stony solitude; when, lo! a sudden turn, and a narrow passage telescopes a dream of scenery. The vista for the moment stuns the eye with the abruptness with which it bursts upon the sight; a blow of beauty. The vision is the Vale of Hope. Castleton clusters immediately below, and the country around spreads a broad picturesque panorama of undulating pastures, white homesteads, and distant hills, all revealed in a sunny light that brings out every distant contour in delicate outline. "It is like passing through the Valley of the Shadow of Death to behold the Promised Land," says Kalmat as he stands entranced against the vast rocky screen that veils the vision from the view of those who have not Faith enough to follow the Narrow Path until the open Heaven of Hope spreads out in rich reward!

The valley of Hope is certainly one of the finest of those Derbyshire Dales whose rich beauty Eliza Cook has sung in enthusiastic verse. Perhaps it is one of the most pleasing vales that English scenery can present. Its fascination lies in its peaceful repose; in its sweet, serene, soothing tranquility —placed in strong contrast with storm-rent rocks, wild uplands, bare peaks, and hungry wind-swept moors. The sun to-day intensifies every line of the scenic contrast, and imparts a gladder green to the breadths of level meadow on which the warm light lies. The little river Nowe ripples in silver curves past white cottages and sheltered farmsteads. There are those harmonious gradations of green—sensitive chords of colour—in the scattered patches of copse, and in the low-lying woods, which belong to the sunny days intervening between the asperity of early Spring and the rich monotonous fulness of Summer. The pastoral peace is at once a picture and a poem.

> "*I found the poems in the fields,
> And only wrote them down,*"

Says John Clare, the poor Northampton poet of Nature. The contrast between the fertile and forbidding, realises in one view "the land flowing with milk and honey" and "the land of gall and wormwood;" and one is inclined to quarrel with the genius of etymology after all, when we find that the word "Hope," in this instance, is derived from the Celtic *hwpp*—a slope, or the side of a hill, instead of having the sweet allegorical signification the Vale suggests, as it smiles on—confident and happy—amid the frowning wilderness and flinty rocks. Not only is it the strong contrast with its savage surroundings that commends this Derbyshire valley. There is also the theatrical suddenness with which its beauty breaks upon the astonished eye. It is a surprise that holds Kalmat captive, as many other people less emotional have been enchained before him. The fertile valley is, perhaps, a mile and a half in breadth. Extending in an easterly direction, for about six miles, it embraces Castleton, Hope, Brough, Bamford, and Hathersage. At Hathersage the Nowe joins the dun-coloured Derwent, where another deep and devious valley intersects the hill country. We cruise the next day about these grey, old-world villages of the valley, sometimes fishing, sometimes sketching, and anchoring for the night at Castleton, just as the last crimson farewell of the sun flushes the west.

And what about Castleton, you ask? There are some show-places you may exhaust in a couple of hours; but to see all that will repay inspection at Castleton demands two or three days. And the expenditure of that time is at once pleasant and profitable. Surely in no other place has Nature so concentrated her curiosities as in this antiquated mite of a town, shut in from the world by the austere hills. Where else is there such a world of wonder in a space so confined? Castleton is a repository of romance. It is a natural museum. Geology in the abstract is an attractive study; but it becomes a passion when pursued amid these Derbyshire rocks and caves. "The fairy tales of science" are here wedded to "the long result of Time." To describe the sights of Castleton, one requires the dimensions of a large volume. Kalmat says that if he were only the Perpetual Curate of Mr. Joseph Hatton's *Valley of Poppies*, it would be the absorbing occupation of his learned leisure to do Castleton descriptive justice. Its history under the Romans, its penal settlement under the Saxons, its association with the proud Peverils, its wonderful caverns, its deep lead mines, its geological and mineralogical revelations, its Shivering Mountain, and its old Castle supply attractive themes for the appreciative pen.

What happy writer was it who, when staying at Niagara, appended to one of his letters the foot-note: "There are some water-falls hereabouts, which are said to be pretty?" In a similar manner, recalling our Castleton experiences, I might remark of the place that there are some caverns there supposed to be curious. For I must—lacking the space of the *Encyclopedia Britannica*—dismiss in a few lines what form the special pride and glory of Castleton. Besides it would be a difficult, if not an impossible task, to say anything new, or even fresh, about a subject so exhausted by a multiplicity of writers who have paraphrased and plagiarised each other. Even the local guide-books cannot " overdo " the Castleton Caverns, although the " high - falutin " reaches rhetorical altitudes too lofty for the safe pursuit of the ordinary follower of the English language, for the most inventive pen, in its most hysterical raptures, would find it impossible to make the weird wonders of these caves more sublime in poetic horror than is the romantic reality. The caverns, be it observed, are not a repetition of one another. While the entrance to the Great Peak Cavern is a stupendous span—a sublimity in stone—a vast vestibule of natural stone-work—a Cyclopean porch, the approach to the Speedwell Mine is but a narrow insignificant passage. The grim, grand portal of the former, however, dwindles down into a mere fissure in the hill; while the threshold of the latter broadens out into a majestic Pantheon-like space that is awesome in its suggestive immensity. And while these two caverns stun the sensitive mind by their solemn grandeur, their Cimmerian gloom, and their constant premonition of the awful Styx and Dante's infernal Ferryman, the Blue John Mine appeals to you by its pure spectacular beauty. It is a series of glistening chambers. Stalactites and crystals make fairy halls. The stony encrustations gleam like a fretwork of frost. Kalmat gives way to the weakness of verse, and says of the guide:

> "*His foot is on the marble floor,*
> *And o'er his head the dazzling spars*
> *Gleam like a firmament of stars.*"

No wonder that the Blue John Mine has been compared to the grotto of Antiparos. The Odin Mine, again, an old obsolete lead working, is interesting because of its historic renown. The Romans worked the lead; and in Saxon times the place became a local Siberia to which prisoners were sentenced to labour out their lives in the mines.

If Castleton is interesting underground, it is none the less attractive above. What an idle, healthful time we spend on the top of Mam Tor, watching the silent shadows sail over hill and hollow, while we discuss the meaning of the name of this shaly, crumbling, "shivering mountain." Does "Mam Tor" mean "rocky height"—derivable from "mor," "maen," or "mannin," the Celtic for rock, and "tor," the Anglo-Saxon for height? Or is it the "mother rock," "mam" being the Celtic for mother or dam? We incline to the latter, for Mam Tor is a hill with such a distinct individuality about it. Over the other hills it assumes a strong maternal command. But why will Kalmat persist in his discussion upon derivatives? He wonders now whether "Tor" is not an abbreviation of "Tower," coming from the Latin *turris*, a tower, and through the Anglo-Saxon *torr*, a tower. And when this dispute is concluded, controversy is again aroused over the remains of the ancient British encampment

on the top of the hill. The frequent shivering of
the shale has taken away most of the camp on the
side facing Castleton; but there is still much of the
double trench to be clearly remarked; and we drink
at the north-east corner of the waters of the perpetual
spring quaffed by thirsty Celt and Roman and
Saxon. The centuries have passed; history has
unrolled its record of good and ill; the whole world
has changed; but still this water sparkles in the
sun an abiding emblem of Eternity. An important
military position this precipitous hill, yet scarcely
more unassailable than the situation of Peveril
Castle, which is only approached from one side of
the crag: that from the south, which is a very
narrow isthmus defended by the keep. The castle
is but a rude shell; but the view from the height of
the concert of mountains and the concentration of
valleys around is not one that will be easily effaced
from our memory. Such mental photographs never
fade. The older they grow, the brighter becomes
their colouring, the distincter the delicacy of their
half-tones, the more decided their touches of light
and shade; and they can be produced at will, years
afterwards, and miles away from where the mental
camera "metagraphed" them upon the memory.
. . . . Kalmat is curious as to the locality of
Sir Walter Scott's scenes in the *Peveril of the Peak*.

He enquires with eager interest for the ruins of Moultrassie Hall, Bridgnorth's residence, and for Martindale Castle, the home of Sir Geoffry Peveril. Where are they indeed? Where are many other ideal places? Where is Utopia? What time is there a train for Arcadia? Where can we find the Happy Valley of Rasselas? Can you direct me to the Elysian Fields? Where is the Idle Lake of Edmund Spenser's *Faërie Queene?* Where, in fact, are all our *Chateaux en Espagne?* I cannot find that Sir Walter Scott ever visited Derbyshire. The local topography of his *Peveril* shows ignorance of the Peake Countrie, although the great Magician has illuminated its hills with his imagination, and invested it with

"*The light that never was on sea or land,*
The consecration and the poet's dream."

Castleton should rather be associated with Lord Byron than Sir Walter Scott. Indeed it was connected with an affecting episode that turned the current of Manfred's miserable life. It saw the rupture of that deep affection which "would have healed feuds in which blood had been shed by our fathers." Castleton is coupled with the breaking of Byron's union with the beautiful Miss Chaworth. Writing of a visit to one of the caverns about this time, the poet remarks: "I had to cross in a boat a stream which flows under a rock so close upon the water, as to admit the boat only to be pushed on by the ferryman (a sort of Charon) who wades at the stern, stooping all the time. The companion of my transit was M. A. C., with whom I had been long in love and never told it, though *she* had discovered it without. I recollect my sensations, but cannot describe them, and it is as well." . . . . And idling on the top of the castle crag in the still sunny air of this emancipated holiday time—with the Hope Valley spreading before us in the full richness of its pastoral beauty, the bleak mountains meeting around, and the deep ravines and the clustering houses of Castleton below—Kalmat talks with some feeling of the effect of the "might have been" on Byron's character, of the noble purpose poisoned, the yearning heart steeled, the generous trust betrayed, the better life blighted. Byron's, alas! is not the only bright career that has been dishonoured by an affection that was a fraud, and a love that was a living lie; and yet his aspiration for Mary Chaworth stands alone, or keeps company only with Dante's passion for Beatrice. . . But a truce to sentiment. It is again a bright June morning; a blithe breeze favours our sails; the steersman is at his place; our harbour dues are paid; and once more we get under weigh for another "cruise on wheels."

Looking at the Ordnance Map of Derbyshire, there is to be seen, some seven miles north of Castleton, a broad and remarkable patch of white, deeply shaded with black. It is distinguished as "The Peak," as if it were an isolated hill, or the North Pole. But the ardent discoverer in search of some solitary eminence towering in austere, ambitious altitude above the rest of its fellows, such as the Government "chartists" have indicated, will be disappointed. The expected mountain giant is not to be found. The expression "The Peak" is a generic title, and comprehends the whole of the hilly country of North Derbyshire, with the encroaching uplands of Staffordshire, Cheshire, and Yorkshire. But it is to the distinctive "Peak" of the Ordnance Survey that we now steer. (Speaking of that map Kalmat is tickled with the curious fact that while "the writing is by J. W. Froggatt"—comes he from Froggatt Edge?—"the hills are by S. Peake!") We meet with but few holidaying mariners in this ocean of heather. Excursion steamers ply not on these unfrequented seas. Aristocratic yachts know not these sheltered rocky havens and deep valley soundings. It is rough voyaging over the billowy roads cut through the heather, and gritstone boulders threaten the bravest springs.

We traverse the exquisite Edale Valley, with the

bold hills rising above the little river, tumbling in white under wooded shade, until we are stopped by the huge steep plateau of Kinder Scout, bounding its whole northern side, a black and morose platform of gritstone even on this joyous June morning, when all the idyllic charms of the opening summer-time are smiling in their soft sweetness over the land. Nowhere, Kalmat admits, could you find a wilder chaos of moor and hill, a more savage sublimity of solitude than among the stern peaks and passes and moorland wastes of this Kinderscout country. He is stunned by the boldness and immensity of the prospect on every side; and we agree in wonder how it is that artists go so far afield in search of sketching grounds, while the moors frowned upon by the Scout, so near and yet so remote, remain practically unpainted. What pictures are presented by these misty crags, and deep water-worn cloughs! Bring thy palette here, disciple of Turner, and give us the gloom and grandeur of these secluded uplands and valleys; give us the wild scenic revelations of Seal Edge and Fairbrook Naze, the strange colours and atmospheric effects of this chaotic upheaval of another world; give us the hidden beauties of Bamford, Derwent, Allport, and Hallam Moors, and the pretty pastoral paths of the Woodlands, and the Highland vale of Ashop. The

Peak has many a magic secret awaiting the touch of thy pencil, and though the paths are rough, and the inns few, Nature affords thee glorious recompense.

By devious and declivitous roads we find ourselves later in the day at the village of Derwent, where the scenery is more soft and sylvan. It is an ideal hamlet among the hills, and after our long cruise we anchor for the night. Derwent Hall is of itself worthy of a special pilgrimage. A picturesque bridge over the Derwent, foaming and brown from the peat moss, gives access to the old mansion, so altered and restored by successive owners that it now resembles Sir John Cutler's silk stockings, which had been so often darned with worsted that no portion of the original fabric remained. Derwent Hall was originally in the possession of the Balguys, a Cheshire family. Afterwards it became the property of the Newdigates; now it is owned by the Duke of Norfolk, who uses it as a shooting box, and has spent recently a sum exceeding £30,000 in adding a new block to the old hall, and decorating the whole. Over the old doorway is the Balguy arms and the date 1672, and the unique ancient oak furniture with which the place abounds dates back five or six hundred years. Such a wonderful collection of genuine old pieces, calculated to drive the least covetous of mortals into sinful envy. The house is crowded from roof to basement with antique furniture collected from all parts of the world by His Grace of Norfolk. Kalmat speculates as to what raptures æsthetic Kensington would work itself over these quaint, artistic wonders. This oak furniture is the real thing, and not the hideous mock medievalism over which Mr. Postlethwaite and the disciples of the "intense" school posture in "consummately utter" delight. Note the tapestry from Worksop Manor, with which the entrance hall is hung, my friend, together with the quaintly carved doors opening to the suites of apartments. What a fine oak chimney piece that is from Norton Hall which enriches the new dining-room, a delightful place with superb carvings, oak ceiling, and diamond-paned windows framing beautiful natural water-colours. I cannot catalogue all the charming old pieces that render Derwent Hall a romance. Here is a marvellous old English four-poster, consummate in carving, bearing the inscription "Rex Carolus I Anno Do 1646;" study these six figures of clever German craft dated 1216; contemplate a cabinet, dated 1634, which would send an ordinary collector crazy; regard this corner receptacle for books and china, inscribed "God with us, 1653," and pause to minutely examine this fine hall settee, with a royal hunting-party carved upon its panels, and dated 1598. A surpassing study for an historic novelist this hall of old furniture. All the cabinets, and even the bedsteads, have hidden drawers that have refused to yield their secrets of family and State in the bygone days of conspiracy and peril. How Sir Walter Scott would have revelled amid all this quaint, suggestive, imaginative upholstery, eloquent of poetry and romance, feud and intrigue, love and revenge.

We spend an idle, careless time in the Derwent Valley, fishing, or sketching, or shooting. It is a country of such a concentrated glory of moor and valley, of old Roman roads and Druidical remains, of ancient barrows, strange tumuli, and rocking stones, of tors and cloughs and scars, that one devoutly hopes that the projected railway, which is to give Sheffield a new route to Manchester, will never break the seclusion of so much sealed charm. Wordsworth was incensed when the locomotive entered the Lakeland, and Mr. Ruskin regards the modern engineer as an emissary of the Evil One, although both poet and art-prophet are answered in the earnest lines of Lord Houghton,—

> "But thou, the Patriarch of these beauteous ways,
> Can'st never grudge that gloomy streets sends out
> The crowded sons of labour, care, and doubt,
> To read these scenes by light of thine own lays."

Still the possibility of the Iron Horse snorting amid the sequestered beauty of the Derwent Valley fills the artistic mind with alarm, and I agree with the eloquent protest of my friend Mr. W. C. Leng, of Sheffield, when he writes:—" You must not tell " anybody that I have failed to work myself into a " state of enthusiasm over the prospect of seeing " the steam horse running wild by the side of the " shimmering Derwent, and waking the echoes of " Millstone Edge with its snorts, and grunts, and " screams. It is a weakness of mind to be senti- " mental, and I doubt whether the æsthetic effect of " a paper mill or two, a few wire mills, a vitriol " manufactory, and an odoriferous tannery, supple- " mented by a dainty manufactory of artificial " manures—inevitable products of progress these " wherever a streak of water and a streak of railway " are found together—would entirely compensate " Sheffielders for the privilege of leaving the old " road between the purple heather and travelling to " Froggatt Edge underground. At present the view " from Millstone Edge is like a glimpse of Eden the " Happy—a vision of beauty—a revelation of loveli- " ness—a thing to dream about—aye, a thing to " thank God for. I have shown it to Scotchmen— " born Highlanders—on days when the axiled light " spread a golden fretwork over the slopes of that " valley within a valley, where hills rise upon the " shoulders of other hills, and where many valleys "meet; and I have heard those Highlanders born "express, in tones touched with emotion, their "enforced praise. Do forgive me, sir, I know I am "behind the times, and I fear that were I a Duke of "Rutland or of Devonshire, I should be like Sir "Hickman Bacon, who when offered a large sum for "a portion of his estate upon which to erect iron- "works and sink a colliery, said, in effect, "Get "thee behind me, Satan." Now do have patience, "and I will recant this fearful heresy of mine ere I "am tied to a stake and burnt alive like my admired "friend the Turk, for being incapable of appreciating "some aspects of our modern civilization. There is "something to be said for putting manufactories in "rows by the side of the now translucent river. At "present the water shines like liquid glass, and has "neither taste nor smell, and the vegetation on its "banks glistens like an emerald; but when the "manufacturers get at the foliage and the water, "these defects will soon be toned down, for they "will toss their sweepings and furnace ashes into "the river to save cartage, will carpet the footpaths "with cinders, and will subdue the verdancy of the "foliage on the trees by smudging it into sobriety."

It would be as difficult to contemplate with composure the money-changers in the Temple as Hathersage made a second Attercliffe, and Grindleford

Bridge a screaming railway junction. There is, however, sweet consolation in knowing that the much agitated "Dore, Hassop, and Castleton Railway" belongs to the distant future, and that the poetical picturesqueness of Derwent's pastoral dale is safe from immediate defacement.

Hathersage and Grindleford Bridge! The names recall glowing memories of our "cruise on wheels." The former old-world village supplied Charlotte Brontë with much of the fine moorland scenery which fascinates the reader in the pages of *Jane Eyre*. The Moor House of that strange, subtle story is still to be seen in the neighbourhood. The vale of Hope is thus referred to in that fine novel:—
" The pebbly bridle-path wound between fern-banks
" first, and then amongst a few of the wildest little
" pasture-fields that ever bordered a wilderness of
" heath. . . . . The purple moors. . . . .
" The hollow vale. . . . . I saw the fascina-
" tion of the locality, I felt the consecration of its
" loneliness: my eye feasted on the outlines of
" swell and sweep—on the mild colouring commu-
" nicated to ridge and dell by moss, by heath-bell,
" by flower-sprinkled turf, by brilliant bracken, and
" mellow granite crag." It should be gratifying to local pride to know that the two greatest lady writers the world has yet produced have largely

drawn their inspiration from the Peak of Derbyshire, for while Currer Bell has given us the moorland solitudes around Hathersage, George Eliot's *Adam Bede* is laid for the most part about Wirksworth. And while Hathersage is connected with literature, it is also linked with legend. The village claims fame as being the birthplace of **Little John**, and the churchyard is said to contain the bones of the Sherwood hero. It is even maintained that the sturdy lieutenant of Robin Hood himself chose the spot where he desired to rest, while he stipulated that his bow and cap should be hung up in the church, when he passed to his rest.

> "*His bow was in the chancel hung;*
> *His last good bolt they drove*
> *Down to the rocke, its measured length,*
> *Westward fra' the grave.*
> *And root and bud this shaft put forth*
> *When spring returned anon;*
> *It grew a tree, and threw a shade,*
> *Where slept staunch Little John,*"

Kalmat is, however, somewhat sceptical concerning the tradition. The antiquaries have certainly agreed to differ over Little John's grave, and it is a "burial question" awaiting settlement. One authority maintains that he died in Scotland; a second that he was hanged near Dublin; while others doubt his existence altogether. Anyhow, Hathersage is the **key to the Robin Hood** Country. Robin Hood's

Hill rises above the vale of Castleton; Robin Hood's Stride is among the scattered tors on Stanton Moor, some rude rocks on Coombs Moss are connected with the valiant outlaw; while Loxley Chase is but a few miles from Hathersage, away in the Rivelin Valley, Hallamshireward. Little John's green cap and bow erst hung up in Hathersage Church; while a sepulchral stone was dug up bearing the conclusive initials "L. J.," which was pointed to with pride by the simple villagers as being those of their forest hero! Mr. John Charles Cox sums up the evidence in the controversy as to Little John's place of burial by saying "the opponents of the accuracy of the "tradition seem to us to have far more difficulties "with which to contend than those who accept it."

All this forms the subject for mighty pleasant discourse as we cruise again down the Derwent Valley to Grindleford Bridge;—now making a *détour* to visit the grand rocky platform of Hu-Gaer ("the city of God") and the Stonehenge-like mysteries of Caelswark ("the work of the Gaels") and to bask on Millstone Edge; then breaking away in the west to climb "Sir William"—one of the most stately and personal hills in the Peak—who rewards the ascent with a surpassing pictorial map, that is what an American would call "a big eyefull of scenery," and in the east to Froggatt Edge, until we are sorely puzzled as to which upland should be awarded the prize for grandeur. Perhaps Froggatt Edge claims the guerdon; but we would dispose of the difficulty like Thackeray did a similar one when visiting the Killarney lakes: "When at the smaller lake, we agreed that it was more beautiful than the large one; then when we came back we said, 'No; the large lake is the more beautiful,' and so, at every point we stopped, we pronounced that particular spot was the prettiest. The fact is *they are too handsome*." Throughout our cruise each hour has given us a fresh picture; we have proceeded from "beauty-spot" to "beauty-spot," and one artist's "bit" has been suddenly surpassed by its successor.

Another day with the sportive little moorland trout, and then we set sail back to Buxton, calling at Eyam, for ever sanctified by Mompesson's sacrifice, and at Tideswell, with its cathedral-like church. The sunset during this return journey burns itself into our memory. It has been a silvery, sunny day of mirthful sparkle, with all the strong, brilliant lights that Paul Veronese loved to introduce in his compositions. As evening comes apace, there is a sight to be seen in the west which must make all men for the moment Sun Worshippers. It is such a spectacular sunset that, if it were thrown upon canvas by a fearless painter of genius, the sages of the Royal

Academy would reject the picture, and Mr. Mahlstick, the art critic, would pronounce it exaggerated, unnatural, and impossible. The western sky is one wild glare of burning red, spreading from north to south, brightening into light, golden wave-ripples, and then deepening to a dusky smoky red again. The vast conflagration of flame gradually fades, until all that is left of its glory is a dim blood-red line against the hill tops. The strong colours—the crimsons and carmines—are loath to let the day die; but they grow restful and weary at last; and an exquisite symphony of faint pale tones enchants us with a sense of tender sadness and gentle repose.

And now, in the moonlight, come the familiar features of Millers Dale, and we pursue the Wye valley up to Buxton, which we begin to regard as not belonging to the Peak at all. Kalmat had thought Derbyshire was done when Matlock and Buxton, Haddon and Chatsworth, were visited; but a new and undiscovered Derbyshire has been opened to us, and he protests that the tourist, who knows the show-places, but is ignorant of the high moorland country of Kinderscout and Castleton, of Ashopton and Hathersage, of Leam and Longshaw, is only in the alphabet of the educational course awaiting him. The tourist is ignorant, too, of the inhabitants.

The character of the people is as fresh and healthy as the scenery. The abusive adage which endows Derbyshire arms with strength at the expense of Derbyshire heads has no application to the shrewd hill-farmers and stolid lead-miners of the High Peak. They appear to speak in aphorisms. When some-one was extolling Charles Lamb as a humourist to Thomas Carlyle, the great philosopher said, "I have known scores of Scotch moorland farmers, who for humour could have blown Lamb into the zenith." This power of caustic humour, expressed in a broad dialect that gives it additional force, is one of the leading characteristics of the lusty, long-headed, loyal-hearted men of the Peak; and it is combined with a cordial warmth of feeling which is all the more noticeable coming, as it does, from rough exteriors and inhospitable hills.

Our ship is paid off; the Whitsuntide cruise is over all too soon; and now the express to the South is to take one of us at least away to the "desk's dead wood." And so we bid adieu to the Peak,

"... *a vain adieu!*
There can be no farewell to scene like thine,
The mind is coloured by thy every hue."

And to-night the piece of Blue John spar revives all the incidents of the holiday, and all the scenes come up for review. The prospect through my window is one of monotonous houses looking dismal in the misty rain, and of dingy streets of slush and mud, with the movement of one or two dripping umbrellas, a cheap funeral, and a melancholy policeman. But what I see is the vale of Hope lying radiant and green under the austere hills. The summer breeze makes an Æolian harp of the stony Windgates. The mountains sketch their shapes before me; the scowling masses of Kinder, with a shaft of strong sunlight athwart their gloom; the haughty peaks of Win and Lose Hills; the familiar features of Mam Tor; the towering shoulders of "Sir William," with the white mist bearding his face. And now come the sweet fresh valleys most dear to the inward eye of Memory: you Ladybower, you romantic Edale, and you fair vale of the Derwent, who can fling the heart's affection for you into words?

FINIS.

SECOND EDITION.

PRICE HALF-A-CROWN.

PILGRIMAGES IN THE PEAK:

Derbyshire Essays.

BY

EDWARD BRADBURY.

("*Strephon.*")

BUXTON: J. C. BATES, and all Booksellers.

Some Opinions of the Press.

A cheery little manual of Derbyshire essays, beginning with the old love-story of Dorothy Vernon, the heroine of Haddon Hall, and wandering thence, by pleasant paths and easy stages, into a district every foot of which Mr. Bradbury evidently knows and venerates. A Week at Buxton is temptingly described; and instructive hints are not wanting for the visitor to this city of health, or to any of the spots in proximity to the Wye, the Derwent, or the Dove. Without pretending to the methodical service of a guide-book, Mr. Bradbury's little volume is a pleasant travelling companion, and a not less acceptable friend of the morning stroll and the evening fireside.—*Daily Telegraph.*

T

Mr. Bradbury rambles here and there, keeping up all the time a running fire of amusing, friendly chat. He has considerable descriptive power. The little book is worth perusal, and visitors to the beautiful scenery in which Derbyshire abounds will do well **to** obtain **it.**—*Graphic*.

An eminently-valuable addition **to** local literature. The writer's descriptive power **is of** the highest order. **He** fairly carries **the** reader with him through the lovely scenery he paints **so** well. A more enjoyable book we have seldom had the pleasure of perusing.—*Brief*.

In "Pilgrimages of **the** Peak: Derbyshire Essays" the author gives us a taste **of** his best quality. **His** first title **is** such **a** good one that it causes **one** to regret that he should have thought fit **to** supplement it with a second. The word "essay" is so typical of boredom in the present day, it is so suggestive **of** pinchbeck sentiment, of second-hand ideas, of tedious verbosity, and platitudinous twaddle—that it **seems a** pity that the additional title was super-added. However, it is ungrateful to quarrel with the picture outside **the** booth when the show within **is** so excellent. In "Strephon" we look in vain for tedious verbosity and platitudinous twaddle, therefore he has no right to entitle his volume "essays." The author has a somewhat rare qualification—he knows what he is writing about; every stick **and** stone, every highway and byway of Derbyshire **he has** at his finger's end, so to speak, before putting **his pen** to paper. Whether he is going **up the** Wye, along the Via Gellia, giving us views of **Matlock,** tearing through the Peak on an express engine, **taking a** Shoemaker's Holiday, sketching on the Banks **of the** Dove, or passing a pleasant Week at Buxton, we are well assured that he is an excellent *cicerone*, who has known all these spots from his youth up, and that his peripatetic discourse will be vastly entertaining. Full of good spirits, with a light hand and a graphic pen, Mr. Bradbury has produced **a very** charming volume. "Pilgrimages in the Peak" will not only **be read in** Derbyshire, but it will **be as** popular elsewhere, **and** it **will** doubtless induce many **to** pay a visit to that picturesque county, and study more closely the beautiful spots the author loves so deeply and **so** well knows how **to** describe. *Sunday Times*.

Of late years the majestic beauty of Derbyshire has received a more adequate **share** of popular appreciation, and the credit of this re-distribution of esteem belongs, first, to the Midland Railway Company for performing the difficult and costly task of burrowing under its crags, and sweeping over its valleys, and secondly to Mr. Bradbury, whose naturally keen perception of the picturesque has been nursed and trained by the incomparable pictures of tor and torrent, dale and purple moorland which constitute "The Peak." As the "Strephon" of the provincial press and the monthly magazines, Mr. Bradbury has made many thousands of people familiar with the character of Derbyshire scenery, who otherwise would have been oblivious of its inviting retreats. "Pilgrimages in the Peak" is the work of the matured artist in words, and places en evidence promise fulfilled and realised. It is not a guide-book disfigured by a reckless shower of inapposite poetry, nor padded out with garrulous anecdote, like a literary wedge to balance an unskilful story. It is a series of finished pen photographs, with a delightful soupçon of romance thrown in, much after the manner of Mr. Black's "Strange Adventures of a Phaeton." The author describes his scenes in a rich and crisp style, clothes traditions with new phraseology, and when he makes a joke—which often occurs—it is worth its natural reward. To Derbyshire tourists the book is almost indispensable; to those who appreciate English scenery it is more than worth its price.—*Public Opinion*.

Another reason for Buxton's growing position is the increased interest that the English people are evincing in the neglected beauties of Derbyshire. The hill and dale scenery of the Peak is almost unrivalled in romantic beauty. Chatsworth and Haddon Hall, Matlock and Rowsley, Dove Dale and Millers Dale, are "fetching" people who know their Switzerland as well as Dr. Johnson knew his Fleet-street. Mr. Edward Bradbury, better known in the provinces by his literary *nom* of "Strephon," has done much to awaken this active appreciation by his picturesque and popular "Pilgrimages in the Peak," one of the happiest departures from guide-book writing it has ever been my pleasure to peruse.—*Society*.

We are constantly being reminded of the vague inscription on the great Egyptian library as to books being "the medicine of the mind." No doubt they are; but to know something of the hygienic chemistry of books, and to apply the medicine, is the main thing. Bearing this in mind, "Pilgrimages in the Peak" can be safely recommended as an excellent restorative for these dull foggy days. It is a series of essays and sketches descriptive of the scenery and traditions of Derbyshire, full of rich imagery, and written in a chatty, crisp style. The author is an artist with an artist's love of the romantic and the picturesque, and never fails to make his readers charmingly interested. "The Story of Dorothy Vernon" is full of deep pathos. "A Visit to the Via Gellia" and "Up the Derbyshire Wye" are as full of poetic fancy as "With the Multitude—a Good Friday Sketch," at Matlock, is humorous. "Through the Peak on the Engine of the Express" might have come from the prolific pen of George Angustus Sala, it is so vivid, and so entirely free from that strained style of descriptive writing now become so common.—*South London Gazette*.

A graphic picture.—*The Globe*.

There are many curious and lovely spots in Derbyshire off the regular track of travel. . . . No writer on the picturesque is more likely to make them known than Mr. Bradbury, who has made himself a reputation as a literary guide to the county. "Strephon" wrote the clever papers on Chatsworth which appeared in the *Magazine of Art*.—*The British Empire*.

Travelling the other day through the beautiful county of Derbyshire, I picked up at Buxton a little volume, entitled "Pilgrimages in the Peak." It is by Mr. E. Bradbury, who writes some capital things, and has a place in several London magazines. The Pilgrimages are descriptive narratives of the lions of the Peak, cleverly written, and they are full of suggestions that are worthy of historical notes. If any of my readers want a holiday, and an idea of thoroughly English character and scenery, they could not do better than take a run through the Peak.—*The Boulevard* (Paris).

A keen appreciation of the beauties of Nature in general, and the beauties of picturesque Derbyshire in particular, is shown in the various descriptions of scenery round about the Peak. We like the chapter headed "Our Week at Buxton" best of all, and the following "bit" vividly recalls certain experiences of our own in that locality. . . . This is very pretty word painting. —Mrs. LEITH-ADAMS in *Kensington*.

A clever young English writer.—*Chicago Times*.

Skill as a literary landscape painter, combined with an intense love of his native county.—*Freemason*.

We have delightful sketches of the Peak of Derbyshire. There is an abundance of antiquarian notes, and such other information as the tourist in those parts requires in order to appreciate the charms of the scenery. Every part of the **ground over** which Mr. Bradbury travels is familiar to him, but **all this might have been** true and the book **might not have been** so interesting to the general reader as **it is.** The author has, in addition to **ample** knowledge, **a real** insight **into the** beauties of the **landsca**pes which **he** describes, **and a** literary style which makes his descriptions breezy and sparkling. We have the story of Dorothy Vernon and **the** traditions **of** Haddon Hall told with great charm **and** spirit.—*Manchester Evening Mail.*

This is a very useful little book. Mr. Bradbury is **by no means a novice at** the work. He displays considera**ble power** of **word** painting, and skilfully interlaces with **his** sketches of notable districts, such references to their leading historical incidents and associations, as to impart quite a charm to its pages. The story of Dorothy Vernon is, of course, told in connection with the account of Haddon Hall, and we may say the tourist in Derbyshire could hardly have a more useful companion than Mr. Bradbury's compact little volume.—*Manchester Courier.*

The **book, "Pilgrimages in** the Peak," opens appropriately with the story, charmingly told, **of** Dorothy Vernon's flight from Haddon Hall. The other articles are vivid and successful sketches of beauty-spots in the Peak, of which Mr. Bradbury is an enthusiastic and poetic admirer. All the places known to fame have been traversed by this pleasant guide, and many a picturesque nook as yet uninvaded by the ordinary tourist or pleasure-seeker is rescued from its ordinary solitude. It must not be thought this is a guide-book, though the author would be one of the most agreeable of cicerones in his native county. He loiters by the brink of the winding Wye, and bathes in the beauty of the dun-coloured Derwent. He pauses in adoration before the majestic High Tor, and gazes with an artist's eye **on** the unfolded loveliness of some grand panorama or the wild luxuriance of some sequestered glen. These he paints with harmonized power and grateful fancy, and it is impossible to avoid the fascination of his enthusiasm. His descriptions are "word paintings," but destitute of "gush." His music is worthy of the theme, but he does not allow his judgment to wander and indulge in misplaced rhapsody. His style is fresh, clear, animated, and attractive. As a descriptive writer he is particularly at home; and in " Pilgrimages in the Peak" some of his best work is seen. He does not rely merely on the fluency of his pen, but expends upon his work patient care, and neglects no interesting detail. His completed efforts give promise of future successes, and we trust he will not rest contented with present laurels.—*Manchester Evening News.*

Mr. Bradbury is a writer who couples with a full appreciation of the charms of beautiful scenery a very easy, unaffected, and agreeable manner of describing them. The work is an excellent guide, and is always pleasant reading—which is more than can be said for many of the guide books.—*Birmingham Daily Mail.*

A gracefully written work, full of vivid descriptions of Derbyshire scenery, word-pictures of the beauteous hills and dales, and rippling brooks, and darksome caverns, and quaint old grey-stone villages that lie sheltering in the quiet valleys of a county that has long been noted for its natural loveliness. It gives a peep at Buxton, and the life the strong and weak lead there, amid crutches, and bath-chairs, and mineral waters; it takes you up the valley of the Wye, past the towers and turrets of Haddon Hall, under whose ivy-clad walls Dorothy Vernon plighted her troth to brave Sir John Manners; it leads you through the dreamy old-fashioned town of Wirksworth, where George Eliot roamed in quest of character, and guides you into the romantic valley of Via Gellia; then, after two glimpses at Matlock, it decoys you to the banks of the Dove, and it is in this charming sketch that the author gives perhaps the most conspicuous evidence of his descriptive power. The little book, which is very prettily got up, with a view of Haddon Hall on the cover, is a valuable addition to the literature dealing with the Peak district, and is a companion that no tourist anxious to see the "beauty spots" of Derbyshire ought to be without.—*Sheffield Independent.*

Mr. Bradbury is out with his "Pilgrimages in the Peak." It is a handsomely got-up little book, adorned with two admirably-executed illustrations, the one being of Haddon Hall and the other of the Concert Hall and Pavilion in the Buxton Gardens. But the best pictures in the book are those from Mr. Bradbury's own artistic pen. He works with a bold and free hand, and his dashing style of treating his subjects is associated with a skill which produces the happiest results. There is decision in every touch of his pen, and in these pen-pictures of his he achieves by a few skilful strokes the success which the artist who works in oil colours finds it passing hard to obtain—light, air, liquidness, distance, the sense of exciting movement as in the rush of the express train, or the rapture of repose as realised in the purple hollow of some Derbyshire moorland by the wanderer who flings himself down there among the heather to enjoy the dreamy quiet of a summer day's still afternoon. "Strephon" has the stuff in him which will enable him to go up higher in the world of literature by-and-by. The careless confidence, and the redundant luxuriousness of some of his passages denote the exuberance of spirit and of strength which is, if a fault, a good fault in a young writer.—*Sheffield Daily Telegraph.*

We may at once say that we like "Strephon's" style of production as exhibited in his latest work "Pilgrimages in the Peak." A lightness of touch, and a delicate yet complete method of treating the scenic beauties of the Peak make the book peculiarly acceptable.—*Nottingham Daily Express.*

No county in England is so rich in the picturesque as Derbyshire; very few have a better show of historical associations. Mr. Bradbury is evidently an admirer of Nature, at once intelligent and enthusiastic, and he has studied the history of his county with diligence and care. These papers of his which come to us in clear type and convenient form, are very interesting, and his companionship amid scenes with which we are familiar is most congenial. He is chatty without being garrulous, racy without being pedantic, and occasionally he is humorous. —*Nottingham Journal.*

Mr. Edward Bradbury is an author possessing a high local reputation, and his work certainly merits all the praise that has been bestowed upon it. To say that he possesses gifts of no mean order is not to advance too much in his behalf, but we may go further than this, and assert that the author of "Pilgrimages in the Peak" is a writer of graphic and original power. It is not every man who writes a book that can be accredited with the faculty of skilful or even adequate literary expression; but Mr. Bradbury communicates what he has to say in a very bright and sparkling way, in short, his method and style are admirably adapted to the subject he deals with. Mr. Bradbury is a man of large information and considerable culture; possessing, too, a warm and vivid imagination and undoubted literary instincts and tastes. Nature never fails to charm him, and in some moods and aspects she moves him as only those who are finely sensitive to her charms can be moved.—*Nottingham Daily Guardian.*

The tourist through Derbyshire could not take with him a more pleasant companion. The writer, in a series of word-pictures, tells, with pardonable pride, of the beauties of the wooded water-valleys, the shady glens, the sparkling streams, and the craggy heights of his native county, and so vivid is his description at times that the reader has no difficulty in accompanying him in imagination in his enjoyable wanderings.—*Yorkshire Post.*

This is a charming little book. We expected that it would be, and we are not disappointed. Individuals who have followed "Strephon" in his wanderings in different parts of the country, know that he does his work well. It is always entertaining, and the mind is improved after being in such company as his sketches provide. Those which refer to Derbyshire have been collected, and they are now presented to the public in a neat little volume brimful of descriptive writing of the most accomplished and delightful character. Every sentence is a picture; every page is a gallery of pictures painted in the imagination by an artist of superior taste, and having almost a divine love of the beautiful.—*Bradford Chronicle and Mail.*

Of the many districts in England to which tourists resort, few are more popular than Derbyshire, and Mr. Edward Bradbury can confidently be recommended as a guide to follow through the Peak. In his "Pilgrimages in the Peak" he does not attempt to deal so much with the historical, archæological, geological, or botanical attractions of the county, as to provide a gossippy, readable companion to its sights. . . . There are many passages exhibiting a powerful grasp of language, attractive word pictures, and a keen perception of character.—*Leeds Mercury.*

The sketches are most accurate in delineation and pleasing in style, and the book is one which will serve as a memento to the tourist in Derbyshire of many enjoyable days spent amidst the romantic scenery so graphically delineated by the author.—*Derby Mercury*.

. . . The book, too, is one that will be generally popular, because of its racy, interesting style of writing. If it is short of one thing, it is in illustration, but the loss is less felt since, to quote a Scotch critic, "the author flings out a sentence, and you have a picture."—*Derbyshire Advertiser*.

Mr. Bradbury wjelds "the pen of a ready writer," which he handles delicately and daintily, and which traces with a fine point the beauties of natural scenery. As a word-painter of mountain, moor, and meadow, dewy vale, silvery stream, and umbrageous wood, he is an artist whose work is worthy of an honourable place in the studio, the boudoir, and the drawing-room.—*Derby Evening Gazette*.

. . . Nay, surely not *Pilgrimages!* There is deception in the term. The severely-decorous reader who proposes to take up this volume in the hope of finding some congenial mental exercise, is doomed to disappointment. There is not the remotest semblance of penance about it. It is composed of nothing more or less than a series of bright, sunshiny sketches, painted by a man who is at once an ardent worshipper of nature and a loyal champion of his county's claims to the romantic and picturesque. It is a literary picture gallery, aglow with life and colour, and profusely decked with touches of real poetic fancy. To ramble with "Strephon" through his beloved valleys, to trudge with him over his eagerly-lauded hills, and wander with him along the meandering banks of the laughing rivulets must serve to exorcise the strain of anxious thought instead of finding material for reproachful meditation. Oh, no, it is not a book for pilgrims. The most gruesome member of the fraternity would be constrained to declare with Mark Tapley that one "couldn't help being jolly" in such companionship. . . . These sketches display an enthusiastic love of the "Peak" for its own sake, a thorough and practical acquaintanceship with its varied characteristics, an excellent literary style, and exceptional taste and skill in the sadly-abused art of scene-painting. The light and shade of Derbyshire landscape—perhaps more diversified and full of contrast than any other of our national pictures—are handled with considerable skill. We know of no artist who surpasses "Strephon" in this respect. Then, in addition to those good qualities we must add the inestimable virtue of knowing when and how to guard against an excess of descriptive power. Mr. Bradbury's sketches are never in the least danger of wearying the most fastidious connoisseur, for the reason that they are not too long nor overcharged with colour.—*Derby Daily Telegraph.*

An elegance of diction and literary gracefulness not surpassed even by Miss Thackeray, who is famous for her descriptions of scenery and her devotion to Art.—*Derbyshire Courier.*

. . . There is something soothing in the easy way the sentences run. The writer's instinctive power of dealing with Dame Nature in her prodigality in the Peak is strikingly manifest here. Many who read this little volume will say with regard to some passages "I have felt all this myself—Strephon delightfully expresses it for me." . . . He is a sincere lover of the beauties of our county, and unlike some lovers his passion makes him eloquent. There seems no part of the manifold varieties of scenery which Derbyshire can show that has not been studied by "Strephon," and his descriptions abound in a wealth of word-painting which brings vividly before us scenes of beauty which it is certain few appreciate so thoroughly as the writer of these sketches. Few probably have studied them so closely.—*Derbyshire Times.*

Fascinating pictures of Derbyshire scenery.—*Leicester Mercury.*

Must make a stranger long to dash off to a Midland station, and ride express to the lovely valleys and immemorial hills.—*Hampshire Telegraph.*

An admirable contribution to the topographical and descriptive literature of the Peak.—*Lancaster Guardian.*

The best narrative we have yet had of the Dorothy Vernon Romance.—*Bolton Journal.*

The sketches are written in a graphic, interesting, and easy style. We heartily recommend everyone who is acquainted with the Derbyshire hills, or who is intending to visit the well-known picturesque and hallowed spots in the Peak district, to read these entertaining descriptions of scenery, and especially the gracefully-told " Story of Dorothy Vernon."—*Leigh Chronicle.*

"Strephon's" descriptive genius has long been dedicated to Derbyshire, and it could have no fairer or worthier mistress. The papers comprising the book, whilst partaking of the nature of a guide to some of the more charming of Nature's pets in the Peak, betray hardly a single characteristic of the common hand-book. The volume is a casket of word-pictures, such as we have been accustomed to expect from "Strephon's" pen. The bulk of the papers are **exquisite descriptive** essays on little **tours** made by chaise **and on foot in** and around the most enchanting haunts **of the Peak, and** the volume is brought to a close with a **most diverting and** graceful sketch, into which **is thrown the lightest vein of romance,** entitled "**Our Week at Buxton."**—*Gloucester Mercury*.

Mr. Bradbury has peculiar gifts as a descriptive writer. He has a keen **eye, not only for** the beauties of Nature and of Art, but for **the** picturesque associations of the places he visits. **Not** only does he describe vividly what he sees, but he has **the** history and antiquities of every locality at his fingers' ends, and he **has**, besides, a fund of literary allusion which **is** eminently useful in **the** lightening up of his bright **and** cheery pages. A more entertaining, **as** well **as informing**, companion, could not be conceived. Descriptive **sketches** are not always **the most** exhilarating of reading, **but** Mr. Bradbury's **volume is**, we repeat, unusually delightful, carrying **the reader** easily along in the irresistible flow of its narration and description.—*Greenock Advertiser*.

Pleasant sketches. . . . Written **in** a desultory and gossipy style, which interests and amuses, whilst conveying those scraps and fag-ends **of** history which the ordinary traveller likes.—*Hastings and St. Leonards Times*.

A charming **essayist.** He **is we** might, without the slightest exaggeration, style the *facile princeps* of pleasant gossipy writers. He is not only a keen observer, but is the most powerful word-painter we have met with for some time.—*Durham County Advertiser*.

Agreeably written, **and** conveys to **the reader** a very pleasant idea **of** the beauties of the Derbyshire spots which it is an act of loyalty on the part of the author to extol. . . . Such **a** fresh and chatty style.—*Bath Herald*.

The press has already been loud in its praise, which we heartily echo. He has a wonderful descriptive power, and presents to his readers powerful word-pictures, almost bringing the scenery of the "Peake Countrie" into view. Others, besides natives and wanderers in Derbyshire, will revel in this delightful little work.—*Boston Independent.*

His book is by no means of local or provincial interest. The Peak of Derbyshire is as much national property as Westminster Abbey or the Tower of London. Its matchless beauty, its gentle charm, its romantic interest, give it this national claim. Mr. Bradbury has written a singularly vivid series of sketches.—*Chelmsford Chronicle.*

To those to whom Derbyshire is as yet a "new and undiscovered country" we would commend "Pilgrimages in the Peak" as the best possible introduction to some of the loveliest landscapes England has to show. Few know the hills and dales of Derbyshire better than "Strephon," and fewer still have the gift of telling what they know with the grace he evinces. "Our Week at Buxton," perhaps the best paper in the book, is an all but perfect example of literary style; and everyone of the so-called "essays" reads like a romance.—*Kent and Sussex Courier.*

Although he does not profess to give us a guide-book, he has produced a volume which would make the best and appropriate companion we know for the tourist in the Peak district, who seeks to know the Peak, and to appreciate it as one of the most perfect of nature's beauty-grounds.—*Essex Herald.*

This delightful little book calls for special notice at our hands. It is dedicated to his Grace the Duke of Rutland, "who has taken a kindly interest in the sketch which tells the old Lochinvar Love Legend of his noble House;" and for that reason alone it deserves a favourable word. But on other grounds, apart from this reference to the Rutland family, are we able to recommend these Peak Pilgrimages to the notice of our readers. Mr. Edward Bradbury, well known by the *nom de plume* of "Strephon," is an author of considerable power and ability, whose charming descriptions of Derbyshire scenery have often enchanted the readers of several of our leading magazines. The glories of the Peak are his own peculiar theme: he portrays them in language of rare beauty, and clothes them with a new and powerful interest—an interest which is simply irresistible. In the book before us, a number of these word-pictures are strung together like so many literary pearls. His descriptive sketches are wonderfully attractive: we can fancy ourselves journeying with him. . . . We are glad to know that the Duke of Rutland has expressed exceptional interest in the book, and has added a copy to his library at Belvoir Castle; and we strongly recommend our readers to follow his Grace's example.—*The Grantham Journal.*

"A charming little volume of breezy sketches."—*Lincoln Gazette.*

A charming collection of graphic sketches of the wild hills and lovely dales of the beautiful Derbyshire Peak. Mr. Bradbury's realistic pen portraiture may almost be said to have the effect of transporting his readers to the scenes he loves so well. He has the grace and gift of a gossiping story-teller, combined with the accuracy of a faithful guide. Those who have yet to behold this beauty-spot of our land cannot have a better introduction than Mr. Bradbury's book; whilst those who have already visited the secluded Peak district will obtain from a perusal of its pages the revivication of many a pleasurable memory.—*Hereford Times.*

In this handsome little book Mr. Edward Bradbury has given a series of very brilliant essays on the Derbyshire Peak, famous as the English Switzerland. The author has dwelt lovingly on the light and shade, the nooks and byeways of the country he describes, and his eye, quick to catch the changing beauty of nature, revels in the varied aspects of hill, valley, and stream which make the Peak region famous. This little volume, however, must not be confounded with guide-books, and yet it is almost indispensable to the tourist; and if he only looks through the eye of its author, he will derive a double pleasure in wandering through the scenery which "Strephon" has so admirably portrayed. He has the quick pen of a prose poet, and photographs as he writes with an accuracy of detail which is very charming.—*Dumfries and Galloway Standard and Advertiser.*

www.ingramcontent.com/pod-product-compliance
Lightning Source LLC
Chambersburg PA
CBHW032046230426
43672CB00009B/1489